Endorsements

For global workers, a good sense of humor is not just a vocational byproduct, it's a survival skill. As I chuckled my way through this treasure trove of personal stories, I fondly recalled some of my own funny—and embarrassing—moments while living overseas (and I confess some of those stories have gotten more exaggerated with time). This delightful book is a gift to anyone who needs reminding that laughter is medicine for the soul, in all seasons.
—**Cindy M. Wu, co-founder and Director of Diaspora Ministries of Mosaic Formation**

Yet We Still Laugh is a beautiful collection of honest, humorous, and hope-filled stories that celebrate the courage of women navigating cross-cultural life and ministry. Through laughter, these women invite us into their bold attempts to embrace new cultures—not by avoiding discomfort, but by leaning into it with joy, humility, and an open heart. Their light-hearted reflections remind us that bravery doesn't always look like grand gestures—it often looks like trying a strange dish, getting lost in translation, or laughing when things go wrong. In these stories, we witness the transformative power of love, kindness, and mutual connection across cultures."
—**Mekdes Haddis, Author of *A Just Mission* and Founder of The Mutuality Lab**

Living cross-culturally can be tragically difficult and also wonderfully beautiful. Often the two go hand in hand, and a little humor can go a long way in not only surviving, but thriving "overseas." In this lovely book, *Yet We Still Laugh*, we are invited to grab a cup of coffee and hear stories from friends–courageous women of God who are giving us the gift of sharing some of their stories. You will laugh and you might cry (I did!) as you enter into this book, and you will certainly be encouraged in your walk with the Lord.

—Anita Rahma, author of *Beyond Our Walls* and *Downward Discipleship*

There is something holy about laughter, cracking open that human side in each of us. Cross-cultural life with language challenges and cultural blunders makes it ripe for a good laugh. What a gift this book is, a reminder not to take ourselves too seriously and to find joy in hard places. I laughed out loud reading these pages. Thank you Velvet Ashes for once again bringing such rich stories.

—Ruth Potinu, author of *Permission to Mourn: Engaging with Culture, Story and Scripture in a Quest for Healing with Hope*

Yet We Still Laugh dives into the beautiful humanity of what it means to live cross-culturally. It encourages the reader with real-life stories, humbling lessons, and an undeniable hope. This book takes differing experiences from around the world and unifies us with one common Hope. God's writing a story from East to West, from heart to heaven.

—Sarah Nunnally, Missionary, Author, and Illustrator of *Every Nation: Seeing God Around the World*

Velvet Ashes has done it again! The authenticity, humor, and humility woven into these stories is a must read for not just women, but also for the men who walk alongside them. Cross-cultural living can be a lot of things...and learning to laugh at ourselves in the process is essential. *Yet We Still Laugh* is not only a humorous and lighthearted read, it's also a collection of worshipful anecdotes from courageous women who learned to thrive in unlikely places.

—**Josh Beck, Executive Director and CEO of Barnabas International**

Yet
We Still

Stories of Humor and Hope from Women
Serving Around the World

Edited By
Sarah Hilkemann, Laura Bowling, and Denise Beck

VELVET ASHES
PUBLISHING

Dedication

"Strength and dignity are her clothing,
and she laughs at the time to come."

Proverbs 31:25 ESV

To the women around the world laughing
despite it all on the hard and holy journey of
cross-cultural life.

Table of Contents

Foreword

By Danielle Wheeler

The Velvet Ashes community was born out of a desire to connect women living the same kind of story. Who else understands what it means to uproot from your life and culture and country and plant yourself in a new and foreign place? Other women who are doing it too.

I'll never forget the bond I felt with the women I went through training with as we entered our cross-cultural life. We shared the same story of support raising and tear-filled goodbyes at airports and all the unknowns of stepping into a completely different life on the other side of the world. After weeks of training together, we all departed for different locations around Asia.

Six months later we reunited at our annual conference. You could identify us all by the befuddled look that comes only in the throes of culture shock. We gripped each other with hugs that went beyond words. After programming was done, we'd find our way to one of our hotel rooms.

Then the stories would start flowing. One after the other, we told each other our cultural blunders, our language mishaps, our embarrassing obtuseness. Each story felt more hilarious than the last. We laughed and we laughed. And I gulped that laughter down like the life-giving medicine it was. My soul unclenched. I was not alone. Endorphins coursed through my body.

Did I need more language learning and cultural training and mentoring? Yes, yes and yes. But perhaps what I needed more than anything else to survive and thrive in this cross-cultural life was... *laughter.*

This book is your equivalent to that late night hotel room full of women. This book is for you if you are preparing for cross-cultural life and want a glimpse of the challenges and hilarity to come. This book is for you if you are in the initial stages of cross-cultural life and desperately need to know, "It's not just me." This book is for you if you are the veteran needing a fresh breath. This book is for you if you're seeking to understand and encourage those in global work.

We global workers take seriously the commission we've been given by Jesus. But what if the seriousness is actually a detriment to the commission itself? Have you ever wondered how it comes across when a bunch of serious, straight-laced, nose-to-the-grindstone kind of people say to the world, "Hey, come join our kingdom?"

Is that us? Or are we a people known by our joy? Does the world look at us and see light and love and laughter? Theologian Karl Barth once said, "Laughter is the closest thing to the grace of God."[1] As you read this book may you laugh—may you chuckle in solidarity, may you bust a gut at the hilarity, may you shake your head at the absurdity, and in this laughter may you experience the grace of God for yourself and for the world.

Introduction

By Denise Beck

Sometimes the stories we laugh at the hardest weren't funny *at all* in the moment. Take, for instance, the time I was in the backseat of a car barreling down some truly awful roads somewhere in Africa. My teammate Eddie was driving—if you can call it that—and my husband was in a different car behind us (why I wasn't riding with him, I simply cannot recall). Eddie tells this story best. He'll start with, "Denise, remember that time I was driving and you were in the back seat? What happened next, Denise? Did you have your phone with you?" And I know exactly where he's going.

Because yes, I did have my phone. And yes, I was so desperate to get out of the situation that I texted my husband a very subtle, very loving message that read: *Eddie is the single worst driver in Africa. Get me out of this car.*

Except.

As soon as I hit send, Eddie's phone—sitting on the center console—lit up.

I had not texted my husband. I had in fact texted *Eddie*. The single worst driver in Africa himself.

What began as an absolute pit in my stomach unraveled into one of the most hysterical moments I've ever experienced. Because there was no way out of it and because Eddie—bless him—was such a good sport, we're still laughing about it today.

In our first book, *Yet We Still Hope*, we invited women to share the real and the hard of cross-cultural life—the unseen valleys, the quiet courage, the relentless holding on. It was honest, raw, and sacred. And now, in this book, we turn the page to something just as holy—laughter. The kind of laughter that bubbles up through language barriers, cultural missteps, unexpected encounters, and the everyday absurdities of life overseas. We believe joy belongs in the narrative too. Joy is a fruit of the Spirit, even—especially—in the chaos.

As I've walked alongside women serving around the world, I've seen a quiet truth unfold again and again: Joy is a survival skill. It is not a frivolous extra; it's a deep well we draw from. Studies say that women laugh 126% more than men.[2] This increased laughter isn't just a quirky fact; it's indicative of resilience. Laughter significantly enhances psychological resilience, reduces stress, and promotes adaptive coping strategies, making it a powerful tool in enduring challenges. Laughter holds communities together, lifts heads in dark seasons, and helps us endure when logic suggests we should give up.[3] [4]

In a world that sometimes values loud over gentle and bold over tender, we forget that it is often the softer qualities like empathy, nurture, joy, and intuition—qualities that can come more naturally for women—that steady a team, a family, a calling.

These are not lesser things. They are sacred tools. And laughter? Laughter in the hands of women is not the sound of uneducated dribble. It is both a medicine and a ministry. In these pages, we celebrate it. Not as a distraction from the hard, but as a beautiful companion to it.

In this book, you'll meet Charissa trekking muddy hills in the Philippines, eight months pregnant, laughing through circumstances she never could've imagined. Amber crashing a wedding with her three kids and somehow discovering grace in the most awkward moments. Rachel unexpectedly befriending a stray dog and transforming an entire neighborhood. And Darlene discovering that laughter and pain can and do beautifully coexist.

Their stories depict the kind of joy I want to honor in these pages. The joy that sneaks up on you. The joy that stitches relationships together and softens truth with grace. The joy that reminds us, over and over again, that God is in the hilarity too. Because somewhere along the way, many of us absorbed the idea that God is only found in the serious, the somber, the hard. But that isn't the full picture. Jesus celebrated. He feasted. He welcomed children. He turned water into wine at a wedding. Joy was never absent from His ministry—nor should it be from ours.

As C. S. Lewis once said to J. R. R. Tolkien, "Tollers, there is too little of what we really like in stories. I am afraid we shall have to try and write some ourselves."[5] So here we are, sharing the stories we long to read. The stories that make us laugh until we cry and remind us that laughter is a part of the sacred journey and that God is in those stories too. The stories that women serving all over the world have been holding.

So welcome, friend. These stories are our invitation to laugh deeply, freely, and maybe even a bit uncontrollably—a reminder that the joy found in ridiculous moments is just as sacred as the quiet ones. As you turn the pages, may you feel the presence of a God who delights in your laughter, who draws near in the absurd, and who gives us joy, not in spite of the mess, but right in the middle of it.

And maybe, just maybe, you will find yourself laughing like I did that day in the car with Eddie—surprised, undone, and completely certain that God was laughing too. Because that kind of laughter? It's not just funny; it's grace. A reminder that even when we get it spectacularly wrong, we're met with kindness, and we're allowed to laugh, to grow, and to carry on.

ANATOMY OF A CROSS-CULTURAL WORKER'S BRAIN

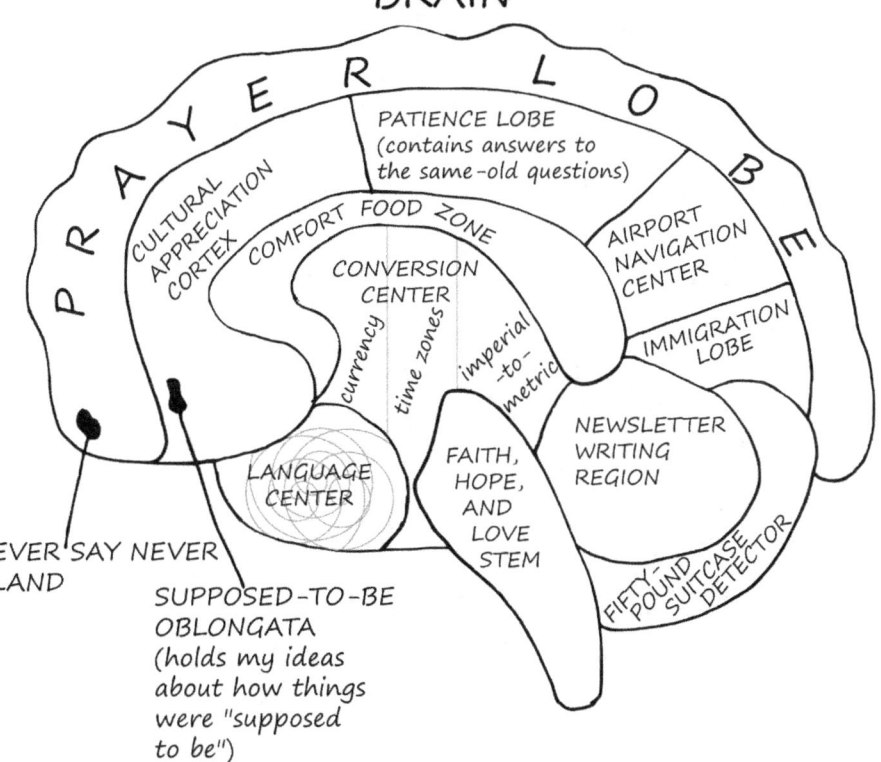

PRAYER LOBE

PATIENCE LOBE
(contains answers to the same-old questions)

CULTURAL APPRECIATION CORTEX

COMFORT FOOD ZONE

CONVERSION CENTER

currency

time zones

imperial -to- metric

AIRPORT NAVIGATION CENTER

IMMIGRATION LOBE

LANGUAGE CENTER

FAITH, HOPE, AND LOVE STEM

NEWSLETTER WRITING REGION

FIFTY POUND SUITCASE DETECTOR

NEVER SAY NEVER LAND

SUPPOSED-TO-BE OBLONGATA
(holds my ideas about how things were "supposed to be")

Section One

Laughter Between Worlds

Laughter Between Worlds

By Sarah Hilkemann

Your bags are packed, you hug your loved ones goodbye, and maybe the tears stream down as you watch that place you've called home disappear, the airplane soaring into the clouds. Your cross-cultural adventure is just beginning.

And then comes the need to put food on the table, navigating a market in a language you don't yet understand. You are offered a local delicacy you can't quite recognize, and you aren't sure what the culturally polite response might be in this situation. You make mistakes and try again and look for ways to belong in this new place that you call home.

Cross-cultural life is full of opportunities to laugh. In fact, I would say being able to laugh is a vital skill to not just survive but thrive.

There's a story I love about Helen Roseveare, missionary doctor to the Democratic Republic of Congo in the 1950s and 60s. Before heading to the field, Helen moved into the Worldwide Evangelisation for Christ (WEC) headquarters to care for a retired missionary in her final days. This was also an opportunity for the organization leaders to evaluate if Helen was a good fit for the field.

PART ONE

Helen never needed to learn housework growing up, but she got hands-on training once she arrived at headquarters. One day she was asked to bring coffee to a meeting, but before carrying it in, she overheard the gentlemen in the room discussing her. *She is stubborn*, they said, *not easy to work with, and she can't do housework.*

Discouraged, Helen asked someone else to take the coffee into the meeting room, and she switched to hanging up freshly washed sheets on the line right outside. As she continued working, she turned around and all those sheets she had worked hard to pin to the line had blown off and ended up in the mud.

Oh, I can just imagine her dismay at this! Sheets are bulky and challenging, and Helen was still learning. But in that moment, Helen sat down in the mud and laughed.

The gentlemen who had just remarked on her stubbornness and challenging qualities happened to look out the window that faced the clothes line. They saw Helen's response and knew that she did actually have what it takes to make it on the mission field.

The key was laughter.

Helen knew how to laugh at herself, to see beyond the frustration of the immediate situation and let go of all the other things she might have been feeling. Her many years on the field were filled with heartbreak, tragedy, and personal loss. Yet Helen was known by her teammates and local friends as a kind, passionate, and enthusiastic woman. She held onto joy through all the frustrating and heavy days.

Humor can be a powerful form of resilience, helping us navigate life's unexpected twists with grace and perspective. When we learn to laugh—at ourselves, at the quirks of life, and even at the moments that don't go as planned—we cultivate a lightheartedness that keeps our hearts open rather than weighed down by frustration or disappointment. A light heart remains teachable, ready to learn and grow rather than becoming rigid. It allows us to continue seeking the Lord with curiosity and trust, embracing all He has for us, even in the midst of life's detours and surprises.

The women who share their stories in this section have crossed borders and language barriers, carrying with them the art of laughter in every hard and crazy situation. This laughter skill has buoyed them as they searched for belonging and embraced the adventure of cultural learning with humility and joy.

As you read the stories that follow, may you be encouraged to embrace the opportunities to laugh not just at the funny moments, but even in the challenges, knowing that joy and resilience often walk hand in hand.

Chapter 1

OUR MOUTHS WERE FILLED WITH LAUGHTER

By Eva Barkholder

I knew when I married my husband that my life would never be boring or dull. He highly values fun, but that wasn't a huge part of my upbringing.

My parents were serious people. Serious about serving as missionary Bible translators and serious about raising me and my siblings to know Jesus. I love and respect my parents who are now with the Lord, but I'm especially grateful for the many "aunts and uncles" and house parents who gave me a taste of, and thus whetted my appetite for, humor and play.

That's what attracted me to my spouse. He makes me laugh. He has a quick, witty, and sometimes sarcastic comeback for every comment. He seeks fun activities to keep life exciting. Our laughter only increased as our family grew. Both our sons and their wives enjoy a good joke and can quickly turn phrase into pun. Over time, I have followed suit and become funnier too. Our home is joyful and full of mirth.

Little did I realize how important these qualities would be when we arrived in Indonesia. I needed my family to help me relax and find humor in difficult circumstances. But God knew we would benefit even more from teammates who also had a keen sense of humor.

Living overseas provided much to laugh about, mostly at ourselves. It began early on the first morning in our new home when the local mosque projected its deafening call to prayer directly into our bedroom. We shot up out of bed, panting—no one had warned us about this! After the shock wore off, we had a good laugh about such a rude, literal awakening.

Within the first month I showed up at a formal wedding in casual clothes without a gift because I had no idea what I had actually been invited to. My ability to make sense of a new language proved unequal to the task.

Killing a rat in the middle of the night with a wooden stick broom was no fun at the time, but we soon embraced the humor in the drama—my husband on one side of the cupboard, me on the other, hoping the offending creature would not run out the other side. Eventually, he struck it over and over in a killing frenzy. So ridiculous.

Then came the day the bed frame collapsed without provocation. Our teammates didn't believe we only lay still upon it, and our bed mishap became the source of jokes for days.

Once I committed the ultimate language blooper in Bahasa when, while recounting the creation story to a new believer, I described Adam as naked and having no genitalia.

And how could I not laugh with joy when my toddler went searching for the perfect mommy on Mother's Day (an activity orchestrated by his father), looked into the sewer ditch, and declared, "She's not in the poopy wadder."

I'll never forget the day our son told us he knew the meaning of the "M" word. Terrified he had figured out our profession and would reveal our carefully guarded cover, imagine our relief when he declared the offending word to be "moron." (Not far off the mark, actually.)

I still chuckle when I think about our first home assignment and my young son's conclusion when he learned that a missionary is someone who goes to another country to tell people about Jesus. "Like us, Mommy?" he replied, "We came to America."

I doubled over in horrified hysterics when my national friend dramatically reenacted her experience with a rat. It ran up her pant leg and dashed around and around her waist until she finally opened her zipper to let it out.

Perhaps the funniest moment of all was our teammate's spontaneous invitation to her "chocolate-chip-oholics anonymous" support group. As she "confessed" her addiction to chocolate chips while clutching a precious bag to her chest and eating them straight out of the bag, we fell on our sides guffawing.

I truly wish I could recount exactly what she said that day. I only know that we laughed until our sides hurt, wiping tears from our eyes. And it felt good, a life-giving relief from the demands of our day-to-day cross-cultural context.

Life was hard. On top of everyday stressors, we navigated team dynamics. We didn't always see eye to eye. We offered our share of apologies. And we said hello and goodbye to a revolving door of colleagues. Our team endured extraordinary challenges from a home break-in with a subsequent stabbing and medical evacuation to religious riots leading to a midnight evacuation. Add to this significant illnesses, mental breakdown, anxiety, and ultimately the deaths of both a teammate and a national coworker.

How did we survive it all? We had times of fun, play, and laughter. They were short, but they were regular, and they were intense. We lived on an island replete with hotel resorts and so many unique swimming pools that our children named each one. We gathered almost weekly at the "bridge, cave, bubble, or golf" pool with any who could join us.

We also visited various beaches or took hikes around local sites. We did touristy things. We showed up at bougie resorts insisting upon local prices to eat, enjoy the pool, and even stay overnight. We celebrated birthdays and holidays together. We played board games. We watched movies. We had fun.

An afternoon by the pool listening to our children imagine and play with each other while we sat and read or chatted and ate fun foods (like chocolate chips) proved paramount for helping us decompress from the struggles of the days before and prepare to tackle the challenges ahead. It broke barriers between us. We could not have survived the stress, let alone the crises, if not for the days we took away from the rings of the phone, the knocks on the door, and the cross-cultural demands of life.

Even though we didn't have a manual to tell us how to do this, I am grateful to God that we innocently stumbled upon our practice of fun and laughter. Research has proven what we learned through experience—our mental and emotional well-being improved; our blood pressure, stress, anger, and anxiety decreased. It strengthened our relationships, relieved our tensions, and thus enhanced our teamwork. I could even make the case that it improved our immune systems (we sure needed that) and added to our lifespan.

God gave this gift to us through my husband, other teammates, our children, and our freedom to laugh at ourselves. I admit that we sometimes gravitated into the realm of making fun of someone on the team or something in our host country, but we tried to keep the jokes only between us and to apologize when necessary.

Despite the challenges we experienced, I believe the psalmist sums up our team life: "Our mouths were filled with laughter, our tongues with songs of joy. Then it was said among the nations, 'The Lord has done great things for them'" (Psalm 126:2 NIV).

If you find a lack of fun or laughter on your team, stop and reflect why this is so. Perhaps you don't have permission to express your silly side. Maybe you fear it will offend others. Possibly you're serious by nature.

I encourage you to find ways to incorporate laughter into your day. Read a joke. Watch comedies or stand-up comedians. Hang out with others who make you laugh. You don't need to have a great sense of humor in order to have fun. Do you like to play games? Charades? Have competitions? Dance? Think of something you enjoyed doing as a child and find a grown-up equivalent.

If you're married, choose something you and your spouse can do together. Include enjoyable activities for the whole family. Invite teammates to join you. Even if they might not consider your activity fun, your laughter and enthusiasm may rub off on them. You might just surprise each other—with joy.

Chapter 2

SWEAT, BURPEES, AND LAUGHTER

By Avery Rose

Having recently moved to a smaller village from a bigger city, I jumped at the chance to get plugged into the community through a fitness class. I was also glad to catch several fish with one net including exercise, language practice, and community connections. Little did I know that Monday, Wednesday, and Friday mornings would be a time when I learned how to laugh with local women and through this laughter become more grounded in communal rhythms.

The first day I attended the fitness class, I was filled with nerves. As an introvert and someone who likes to do things well, starting a new activity is usually daunting. Add a good dose of cultural and language differences, and stress was the byproduct. I put my workout clothes in a bag despite my trepidations and walked fifteen minutes from my new apartment to an unassuming small building situated between the bank, a fried chicken place, and a guest house that doubled as a café.

Entering the makeshift fitness center, I stumbled through the small locker room, figuring out where to change and put my stuff. Then I found a place to awkwardly stand in the fitness space while waiting for the class to start. A wall of mirrors, dumbbells in a corner, yoga mats rolled in another, a few house plants, peeling carpet, unplugged AC units, despite the climbing summer temperature, and a Mickey Mouse comic pasted on the wall made up the space where I would slowly become a part of this community. At that moment though, finding community and belonging felt like a distant hope. I glued my feet to the floor and encouraged myself to push through the awkwardness even as my brain said to turn around and leave.

I gathered that the instructor was running late, but someone was assigned to connect a phone to a Bluetooth speaker and begin the class. The women danced the familiar-to-them-but-brand-new-to-me Zumba warmup routine. As anyone who has learned a new dance in a room full of people who already know the moves, I felt lost in a sea where everyone else belonged.

They all went right while I moved left. Again. *What am I doing here?* I thought to myself. The self-doubt that often floods my brain as an expat came rolling in again. I tried to speak the truth, reminding myself that doing something new usually means making mistakes. Between exercises, I stood uncomfortably trying to dig up the courage to speak or even to simply ask the woman next to me her name.

The first few times, maybe even the first few dozen times, of going to these fitness classes were painstaking. For the initial weeks, it was my big, adventurous thing for the day. I think what kept me going was the need for routine and consistency. The trainer's policy on attendance was also a big encouragement. For every class a student misses, they have to do a hundred burpees (without a pushup), and tardiness costs fifty. I learned the verb "to pay off a debt" this way. My trainer even has a whiteboard where she keeps track of who owes her how many burpees. Slowly, through this class, this group of women became the place in my host community where I came alive and learned to laugh.

The next brave thing was attending a dinner for one of the women in my group. To this day, I do not know what we were celebrating, as I missed the initial conversation when the party was being organized. (I believe it was either because my classmate was building a new house or starting a new business.) I had been attending classes for about two weeks when my classmate announced the party. Thankfully, I caught enough of the details to understand when and where the party was taking place. As we ate the traditional Central Asian dinner consisting of food, sweets, and drinks covering every inch of the table, I realized I might need to give a toast. I had no idea what I was toasting, but I knew how to come up with a generic yet sincere toast. That night I also learned a bit more about some of my classmates and was able to share a bit more about myself.

As I continued to go to class, I realized this space our trainer created is a beautiful place for people to be themselves. In their world, which often involves women minimizing themselves and caring for the needs of husbands and children, my classmates are able to let their guard down and just be, and laughter is a huge part of that. It's the small, knowing shared grin between a classmate and myself as we both move in the wrong direction during Zumba. It's being able to move and care for our bodies, laughing as we do hip circles and pelvic floor exercises together. It's the shared comradery paying our burpee debts or scheming how to make the exercises easier.

Initially, I often felt I was being laughed at by the other women in the class. To some degree this speaks to my self-consciousness and wanting to be seen as good and correct. There is also an element of my host culture at play. In some ways, gentle teasing can be a form of love or affection. This was not completely new to me as my family of origin functions similarly.

This understanding changed during a moment of realization as I was doing an exercise involving battle ropes, which we did every week. One of my classmates began to describe that I swung the ropes like I was riding a horse. Initially I was offended—I was working hard to do the exercise correctly. I took a breath and paused for a second and realized she was describing how others (and even herself) did the exercise. This was her way of including me. I joined in, laughing and agreeing with her assessment.

From that moment of realization, I was considered a part of the group and not simply the weird American girl stumbling over words and exercises. My confidence grew. I attempted to participate more in conversation. I even started making my own jokes. One morning, during a cardio workout where the trainer had us alternate between a minute of running and a minute of cardio exercises, one of my classmates joked that running was what all Americans do in the morning. I replied, saying she was living the American dream.

Afterward, I asked her how she liked her American dream morning. She told me she was not a fan. Another time, my trainer lost track of whether we had completed both the right and left sides for an exercise, accidentally asking if we had done the third leg. We all chuckled. Later, when we were finishing an exercise on our right and left leg, I interjected, "Now, we'll do the third leg."

There are still moments of misunderstanding and a tired brain trying to keep up with conversation while simultaneously gulping enough oxygen to continue, but I find myself belonging more to this group of women. We have a lot that could separate us, but laughter and shared humanity as women knit us together. This community shares life together. I've been to baby showers and funerals for the women in this group. Nutrition tips and places to buy new shoes are shared. Laughter and sweat intermingle in this bond of sisterhood that transcends culture.

Reflecting on the sweet memories shared with these women and the anticipation of more to come reminds me of the solidarity of doing hard things together which brings joy and strengthens connections. As I share humor and smiles with these beautiful women, I pray for them to know the heart of our Eternal Father, who smiles over them and dearly wants them to come to Him.

Chapter 3

LANGUAGE LEARNING IS FUN!

By Chris D.

A story from my early days of language learning has become a running joke in our family whenever the topic of shopping for lettuce at the market comes up.

Many, many, well, many years ago, after we had just arrived on the field in the midst of the hottest season of the year, the daunting task of learning the national language with five tones and an indecipherable script lay ahead of us. My husband signed up for a language school in the middle of downtown, so he had to leave our rental townhouse in the suburbs before the crack of dawn to catch the bus before 6 A.M. Only by leaving this early was he successful in placing one hand on the rail and one foot on the steps of the overcrowded bus, hanging on for dear life as millions of people in the capital made their way to work in the early morning rush hour.

As we had a four-month-old baby, attending language school was out of the question for me. With no nanny and new to the neighborhood, I decided to stay at home.

After asking two of my colleagues if they could recommend a language teacher who would come to my house, I set up lessons with two different teachers who came on alternating days. One was an elderly lady, reserved and refined, who had tutored generations of cross-cultural workers from various organizations in the capital. She was very structured, speaking clearly and slowly to make sure I could follow. The material was based on the same book that my husband was studying at language school.

The other lady was quite vivacious. She rang the bell, came in, sat down, and asked: "What shall we talk about today?" Pointing at various pieces of furniture and objects in my living room, she said, "This is a chair; this is a table; this is . . ." Overwhelmed with tons of words that I had a hard time scribbling down, my vocabulary tank filled rather quickly. When she got impatient with my slowness, she would grab my pencil and my notebook and write the words down herself. By the end of the first week, I had studied the phrases, "How much is a kilogram of . . . ?" and "I want one kilogram of . . ."

My homework assignment was to go out and practice in a real-life situation. So with trembling knees, off I went to the local wet market. Taking my baby along in a kangaroo-style carrying pouch, I trudged along the dusty, hot street towards the market. Needless to say, a blonde foreigner carrying her baby in the heat of the day in hot season caused quite a few whispers and stares.

Not having enough words to start or carry on a conversation,

I just nodded and smiled and finally made my way to the nearby market unhindered. The large hall with its tin roof was mercifully shaded, so I took my time browsing and looking at all the vegetables and fruit. So many unknown items, I should have brought my new picture cookbook! Finally, after circling all the stalls for the umpteenth time, I decided to meet the inevitable head on.

A vendor generously sprinkling water over the greens displayed on a large stand in front of her looked nice enough. Since we love to eat green lettuce, I decided that this was the place to practice my homework sentences. I smiled, nervously glanced at my crumpled piece of paper a few times, and managed to say the first sentence.

The vendor smiled at me (she had understood!) and named the price (equivalent of half a dollar/euro). I remember thinking to myself, *Wow, now that's quite cheap*, and before my courage left me, I squeezed out my next sentence: "I want one kilogram of lettuce!" (At this point I did not know the refined way of saying, "I would like," but I did add "Please" after my order.)

Without missing a beat, the vendor bent down, rummaged behind her stall for what seemed like minutes, and emerged with a huge plastic bag. When she started stuffing more and more and more of the leafy lettuce into this huge bag, I was flabbergasted that I had not taken the pains to be prepared and studied words like *no, thanks, this is enough, just a handful, stop please!* So with a red face I accepted the huge plastic bag, paid my ridiculously little money, and started my arduous walk back home in the scorching heat, toting not only my baby but also a huge bag of lettuce.

Mercifully, I had no clue what the ladies I met on the way back were whispering to each other, shaking their heads about this strange foreigner. Well, this joke's on me! Even years later, as we talk around the dinner table or attempt to entertain some guests, the story has been told endless times: "Remember when Mom brought home this huge plastic bag full of lettuce??!!"

During classes in pre-field training we had been told, or rather drilled, that while learning another language as an adult, you have to learn to laugh about yourself. Well, I did once the embarrassment faded and I was able to see the humor in it. Later I was able to use that story many times when I met newcomers who were struggling through their first steps in language learning. Sharing my "lettuce story" helped them feel not so awkward in their own challenges.

But as a result of that first language learning lettuce purchase, I kept going back to that vendor over the following weeks and months to purchase my vegetables, practicing my sentences and returning home with successful purchases of reasonable amounts of items, until we had to move to a different district in town. Over time, my language skills did improve somewhat. The vendor would be on the lookout for me, see me approach, and smile broadly. Then when everything was weighed, put into the inevitable thin plastic bags (which were later used as garbage bags), and all the individual prices tallied up on an oversized calculator, she sometimes added a piece of veggie or fruit into my bags as a special favor to a VIP customer.

The people in our country of service smile a lot as their way of life, and it definitely defuses embarrassing situations or potential crises. Even when they did not understand my attempts in using their language, they would still smile. The only problem is the moment I step out of the plane for a time of home assignment and people in my passport country, in contrast, seem to always be so serious and intense and—dare I say—unfriendly? They would roughly say to me: "What's that stupid smirk on your face? What are you grinning about? Are you making fun of me?" But that's a different story for another time.

As Proverbs 17:22 says, "A joyful heart is good medicine" (ESV). I'm trying to remind myself to take a spoonful of that medicine each day and share the gift of a smile with the people I meet on my way.

Chapter 4

THE TERRIBLE, HORRIBLE, NO GOOD, VERY BAD GETAWAY

By Janessa Cypher

We don't leave our home in the northern Uganda bush very often, but when we do, I tend to have a few expectations for the trip. On one particular getaway to Kampala, I had hoped for at least some rest and relaxation in between all the pre-planned errands that needed to be done.

However, I soon discovered it would be a terrible, horrible, no good, very bad getaway.

After a seven-hour drive, my husband offered to take our three kiddos to swim in the little pool while I settled into the Airbnb. Unfortunately, our four-year-old swallowed a mouthful of water and threw it back up. Then my eldest son shouted that there was a dead rat at the bottom of the pool. Thankfully, the dead rat was actually a water-logged leaf. The panic in my chest lessened as they relayed the story to me, but I never could seem to get that image out of my head.

We decided we wouldn't be going back to the kiddie pool anytime soon—terrible!

Later that evening, we decided to order from Pizza Hut because it tasted like "home," but our online order for a large pizza was canceled four times. My husband eventually gave up and drove to KFC for takeaway. When he returned, a delivery guy called to tell us he had arrived with our Pizza Hut order. We feared we would receive four large pizzas, but thankfully it was only one. The pizza, however, was cold.

Then, in the middle of the night, we were awakened by our oldest who said his brother had thrown up in bed. Plus, their little sister kicked them in the back all night long, so no one slept well—horrible!

In the morning, my husband left to run a few errands. Forty-five minutes later he called from the parking lot to tell me that our "new" thirty-year-old vehicle hadn't started. At the ninety-minute mark, the children shouted that the mechanic had arrived. We were very thankful when the vehicle was fixed and my husband finally left the parking lot. Woefully, he called us ten minutes later saying the vehicle wouldn't start up again. The kids and I spent the rest of the day streaming movies because I had told the kids they didn't need to pack any toys for the trip.

They wouldn't have any time to play with toys, or so I had thought—no good!

I tried to sit outside on the balcony to enjoy the scenery, but a noisy weed whacker below started up, and it was so loud I couldn't think. A few minutes later, a friend called wanting to meet up with us for dinner and a movie later that evening. Six hours later, my husband returned with a working vehicle, but nothing else had been accomplished. The kids and I were excited to watch a new movie at the movie theater, despite the fact that we had watched nothing but movies all day long.

Our friend, however, had waited longer than expected for us to arrive at the mall and no longer wanted to see the movie. The kids were disappointed, but I gave them "the look," and they managed to pull it together. We ate hamburgers, fried fish, and a Philly cheesesteak for dinner as we chatted. My husband and I decided to make a detour before heading to the Airbnb and surprised the kids with the biggest brownie sundae they had ever seen. We couldn't wait to make some good memories on this little getaway. In no time, we demolished every morsel and headed back to the Airbnb for the night.

As I went to give goodnight kisses, my kids scared me with an ugly chicken mask they had bought with their dad. I was not a fan of being scared by an ugly chicken mask or a fan of being scared at all. Then, when all was calm and quiet, everyone was startled awake by a strange noise. We discovered our youngest son had thrown up again and had targeted his little sister's legs. She sat there in silent disgust, so I quickly cleaned her up and stripped the bed again. To this day, I have no idea why we let him choose fish for dinner or encouraged an impromptu chocolate ice cream party right before bed—very bad! (But that one was on us.)

Unfortunately, the following morning, the cycle started over. As I entered the bathroom, I stepped on a huge cockroach and nearly lost my mind. Then, without skipping a beat, my middle child managed to scare me again. He had hid outside the door with the awful chicken mask, and I accidentally smacked him right in the chicken face! I felt bad but also really annoyed that the chicken mask still made me jump—terrible!

We decided after another rough night that we would skip all the errands for the sake of family fun and go see a movie. Surprisingly, we made it in time to watch the previews, and I grabbed a much needed iced coffee to bring in with me. But halfway through the show, my husband wasn't feeling well and went to lay down in the vehicle. After the movie, I had arranged to have a haircut at a place nearby, so the kids and my husband drove back to the apartment without me.

Nevertheless, once they had arrived at the Airbnb, we discovered the keys were with me. So I jumped on a motorcycle taxi and sat sidesaddle as we weaved in and out of heavy traffic because I had worn a dress. I wasn't planning to ride through a busy city on two wheels that particular day, and to make matters worse, the driver took me to the wrong place. The children were very grumpy when I arrived, and my husband went straight to bed. He ended up testing positive for malaria—horrible!

We decided my haircut would have to wait, so I took the kids to the pool. Not the kiddie pool, but the other pool—the one without leaves that looked like drowned rats. We got to the pool, and it was a much better experience. But, the milk from my iced mocha didn't sit well with me, and I suddenly needed a bathroom. To my delight, there was a bathroom close by; however, there was no toilet paper. I managed to scrounge up a few pieces of (I hoped) unused Kleenex that were smashed in the bottom of my purse—no good!

When we returned from swimming, I was annoyed to discover that the kitchen was completely flooded. Apparently, I had forgotten to tighten the cap on a five-liter jug of drinking water left in the fridge, and it had been leaking out for the past hour—very bad!

It had not been my kind of getaway.

When we woke up on our last morning in the big city, we decided I needed to lighten my hairy load. The haircut went well, and I asked to use the restroom afterwards. Unfortunately, as I opened the door, I was soaked by water shooting out from a dirty, busted pipe in the wall. I stumbled backwards into an employee passing by and mumbled something about there being a problem. As I tried to explain, I looked down and saw water had leaked out into the hallway. Too bad I hadn't seen that puddle before I had walked in—terrible!

I tried to dry myself off a little before I walked over to the restaurant where my family was. A familiar voice shouted, "Mom! You forgot to change out of your pajamas!" My middle child stood in front of the restaurant and declared to all of Uganda that I had forgotten to get dressed in real clothes that morning. I calmly tried to explain in a hushed tone that I was dressed in my comfy clothes for the long car ride home. But when I thought about it later, I was sure I had worn those pants and t-shirt to bed at some point, so he wasn't entirely wrong—horrible!

As we drove home, I smiled at my husband and remarked that it had truly been a terrible, horrible, no good, very bad getaway. I was almost ready to move back to North America. We both laughed and recounted the humorous moments of our Kampala trip. He agreed that it had been a rough few days but reminded me that some getaways are like this.

Even those that happen in North America.

Chapter 5

WHO IS MY NEIGHBOR?

By Darlene Grace

We all expect to make cultural bloopers in our host country, especially when we are newcomers on a steep learning curve. I, on the other hand, have become quite adept at making cultural blunders in my own passport country. In the face of possible humiliation, however, I choose laughter.

Switching between our mountaintop home in the East and our passport country in the West was like moving between two different planets. Culturally, the two were complete opposites in many ways. We loved the people and culture of our mountaintop area, but we also enjoyed being back in our passport country with our family and friends. The problem was remembering which place we were in and how to behave appropriately!

One time we were visiting a dear, elderly couple with our five children in tow when suddenly, the host stood up and offered to get us drinks. Without even a moment's hesitation, I politely replied, "No, no! Don't go to any trouble for us." Surprised, the woman sat down, and the conversation continued for another hour or so until it was time to leave. We would have loved drinks, but strangely, our hostess never went back to the kitchen to get them. On our departure, we walked past the kitchen and happened to glance in. What a sight! A feast of dozens of delicious cakes and biscuits was beautifully laid out on pretty plates. Oh, how we wanted that food and the drinks she had on offer. But she had only asked us once!

It was a lesson in being mindful about which culture we are in. When it comes to hospitality in our passport country, we are supposed to gladly accept drinks and food. But in our mountaintop host country, it was polite to decline all hospitality multiple times, while at the same time, the host would be bringing out the drinks and food for the guests, regardless.

On another occasion I had some sheepskin slippers that needed restitching. I didn't expect any problems in my passport country (nor would I have expected any problems in my host country). But I was mistaken! How hard can it be to get a simple slipper repair? It's easy, unless you behave weirdly, like someone who lives on another planet.

The man handed me the repaired slipper as he announced the price. "Five dollars, please," he said in a cheery voice. *Five dollars!* I couldn't believe it. I always paid twenty cents to the shoe repairers on the streets in our mountain home. "Can you make it cheaper?" I ventured. The man stared at me incredulously before finally saying, "No one has ever asked me that before." At that moment I realized what country I was in. We don't bargain here; we don't haggle over prices. We just pay up and get out. I fumbled in my purse, found the money, and thanked the man before making a hasty departure.

While cultural bloopers may at the time feel a bit awkward or humiliating, they are marvelous sources of laughter afterwards. We've all gone through the humiliation of learning a new language or two and at the beginning knowing only enough to speak as well as a small child. But back in our passport countries, we think we know how to operate. It's a culture, after all, that we are supposed to know. The problem is that in the few years we are away, things change. New words even come in that everyone knows except us. And that's what caught me out at the supermarket.

There I was waiting to pay for my groceries with my credit card. A simple and easy transaction that should have caused no problems. But not for me! The cashier looked at me and asked, "One Card?" What a bizarre question. Somewhat confused, I replied, "Yes, one card: my credit card." But she wasn't happy with that. She kept pushing me for a response to "One Card?" What on earth was she talking about? Finally, I conceded, "Sorry, I don't know what you are talking about." There was no response. She just completed the transaction, and I paid with my credit card, wondering what that question had been all about.

I soon discovered that "One Card" was the name of the supermarket's discount card. The supermarket chain was spread throughout our passport country. Everyone who lived there knew what it was. If she had asked in the language of my mountaintop people if I had a "discount card," I would have totally understood her. Or even in English it might have worked. But when you are already paying with one card—Visa—what's another "one card" for?

Navigating two different worlds was equally perplexing for our young and growing children. And who's to blame them if their parents can't even get it right? My husband mentioned something about the neighbor who was outside to our young son. He looked at her and said adamantly, "She's not our neighbor!" Puzzled, my husband asked, "Why do you say that?" Without any hesitation our son replied, "She's not Asian. Our neighbors are Asian!" Well, in our mountaintop home our neighbors were Asian but not in our passport country. Our son had tied a nationality to the word *neighbor*.

A few years later in a different town, our young daughter was equally confused about the neighbors. She came into the house one morning to tell me excitedly that she had seen the neighbors across the street and they weren't foreigners! Now I was confused. "What do you mean?" I asked. "Well, they aren't foreigners like us!" We were in our passport country, in the town I grew up in, and she thought we were *foreigners*! She had tied a nationality to the word *foreigner*. In her mind foreigners were always Caucasian, and locals were always Asian. In a different country things get switched around. And it turned out that our Asian neighbors were also locals, not foreigners. How confusing is that for a child to understand.

One of the beauties of knowing multiple languages as a family is that you can incorporate extra words from the host languages into your family lingo. Words that just don't seem to have an English equivalent. Words that are just good fun to use. It added a richness to our family vocabulary and probably further bonded our family as uniquely strange. We had to always remember to keep those words out of conversations with our family and friends in our passport country. But with our expatriate friends in our host country, they totally understood and used them too.

The problem was with five children, not all of them seemed to get the message about which words were English and which were not. One day our twelve-year-old daughter came home and demanded to know why we hadn't told her that *mabu* wasn't English! She was at a friend's house and had asked for the *mabu*. The friend was totally puzzled, but they eventually worked it out. And our daughter learned the words *kitchen cloth*. What a complicated—but fun—world we live in. As long as we remember to enjoy the ride and laugh a lot!

Chapter 6

RULES FOR FARTS AND PUTTING ON A SARI

By Gwen Elm

No matter how good of a culture student you are, there will always be things that you miss. There are nuances that children learn from their mom and dad that are too awkward and perhaps shameful to discuss openly no matter how many questions you might ask about them. I have learned that no aspects feel more personal, are harder to discuss, or breed more shame than the ones involving bodily functions.

We sat down on some worn cushions for hot tea with a few longtime friends. We were talking about life and particularly health issues. Health issues are not private; Nepalis discuss their own and others' health challenges freely and openly. I had never met someone who felt any shame about any medical condition, save infertility.

While sharing quite seriously about a recent surgery and complicated recovery that my friend's dad was in the middle of, he kept going out of the room for a few seconds and returning. I could not figure out what was going on. Then there was a passing comment about his stomach feeling upset from some bad dumplings he had eaten the night before. A light went on. He was going out of the room to let off some gas! Instantly I pieced together a social rule and all the times I had violated it with some silent but deadly ones I had let off at various social events.

The discovery of a social rule and subsequent reflection occurred almost instantly for me, but my husband didn't quite catch on. Four more times our friend left and returned, and finally, Ezra spoke up. "Are you okay? Do you need to do something?" he asked rather directly. We saw the instant bleed of red creep up from his neck to his face as our friend said, "No, no. I'm fine." Ezra, feeling concern for his friend, pushed it a little further, and I could see the redness deepen. "He's just not feeling well. Now tell us more about your father's follow-up," I said, trying to divert and change the subject. This was followed by a look that I hoped communicated to my husband that he should drop it.

It wasn't until our friends left that I told Ezra about my discovery, and we talked about all the times we had seen this rule in play. This was a rule that no friend would ever talk about or tell us because it could be a source of immense embarrassment. However, we're not naive enough to simply assume a cultural rule without asking our closest friend, Ram, about it. Even bringing up our experience and subsequent discovery brought redness to Ram's face. He confirmed: If you need to make a stink, you should step outside.

Some cultural rules are most appropriately taught by parents. And you should not let any silent ones slip out in the presence of others.

Would you believe that another such rule is learned by every girl at a young age: how to change appropriately in front of others.

I grew up in American public schools. I grew up with gym class, locker rooms, and changing quickly and discreetly in front of others. It wasn't something I was accustomed to feeling shame over as long as I was surrounded by women.

I was a student of culture enough to know that the Nepali standard for modesty was different from my passport country. The Nepali standard is largely more conservative with thicker straps and covered thighs. I was shocked the first time I encountered completely open breastfeeding and the time I first saw women wearing saris and bearing their midriffs of varying sizes.

Then the occasion came for me to don my first sari. I had spent months trying to make a friend my age. Most women in their twenties were married off and under the thumb of their mother-in-law. They were busy all day doing the washing, cooking, and housework, as well as bearing and tending to children. Finding someone my age with free time took a lot of work, but I finally found a young mom who had married a middle son and didn't have to live with his family. Sure, she was busy throughout the day, but Sujaan let me hang around.

Her brother was getting married, and she invited us not just to the party palace affair but also to the parade and procession

54

around town and more intimate family Hindu ceremony that was happening the day before. This meant two days altogether and two different saris that I was going to need to procure and wear.

Even though the invitation was last minute, I had no trouble getting my saris tailored. I just had no idea how to put one on so that it wouldn't immediately fall off. All I could think about was the walking procession from the bride's house to the groom's. I knew that if I didn't tie my sari well, then at some point there was going to be an embarrassing wardrobe malfunction.

To my relief, we were invited to Sujaan's parents' house extra early to meet the rest of her family. She said that I could just change into my clothes with her and her sisters.

We went over early, saw some of her childhood home, and shared many cups of tea. Then it was time to get ready. I went into the small bedroom with five other grown women to put on our fancy saris. I don't know if it was because no one wanted to change in front of me or if it was decided that I would need the most help or if no one wanted to sit in their saris longer than they had to, but it was decided that I would get dressed first.

Not to be one to make things awkward, I just decided to go for it. I laid out the petticoat and the blouse. I took off my kurta top to put the blouse on in quick high school locker room-like precision. Sujaan securely tied the back for me. The next piece to put on was the long petticoat. Again, with quick high school locker room-like fashion I stripped off my leggings to put on the petticoat.

I had one leg out of my leggings and my underwear fully exposed when there was a collective gasp that escaped from every mouth in the room. Did I step in something? Did I have something on my backside I didn't know about? Was my skin really so white and blinding? I had no idea what to think and why I suddenly felt a deep sense of shame with one leg in some pants and one leg getting a nice chill. Suddenly Sujaan let me know that I was supposed to put my petticoat on first and then discreetly slip out of my leggings.

But by that point it was too late. Having one leg out of the leggings meant that I might as well just take the other out and put the petticoat on rather than dancing around the room trying to negotiate half a pair of leggings and a long petticoat.

What was done was done. I could sit in shame the rest of the day and feel awkward about my most exposing cultural blunder, or I could commit to never making that mistake again and move on. All I could think was that I'd given this whole family something to talk about whenever they got together to get ready for a family event—the day they saw the whitest thighs they were ever going to see from the girl who had absolutely no shame stripping down in front of others.

Chapter 7

LAUGHTER AND LESSONS OVER THE RICE POT

By Caroline Found

Food gives many opportunities for laughter, especially as cross-cultural workers navigate the surprises and delights of new and different foods. Making chapati: Even after seven years, mine still look more like a cartoon-shaped "splat" compared to the women I share life with who make perfectly circular ones. My first efforts at dealing with a coconut: How do you open one? Too proud to ask, I spent some time throwing it on the cement floor to try and break it open before I realized that the fibrous husk needs removing first. I don't think anyone saw me!

But laughter over food has also taught me so much and helped in my journey from my home in the U.K. to India. Laughter is a great teacher. The following story happened early in my journey while I was still in the U.K.

It seemed like a good idea before we started: to take a group of families from different nations to enjoy the English countryside and cook them all an easy one pot (well, two) dish. What could be easier than a few English women (with limited expertise in my case) cooking a big pot of curry and rice for a group of Asian women and their families? I mean, curry can't be that hard, can it? And surely you just boil rice, right? *What were we thinking?*

We were beginning to connect with and care for these families, all seeking refuge in the U.K. and sent to our small town while their various cases were considered. Offering friendship and practical help, we were a group of enthusiastic church planters seeking to befriend, care for, and share with those new in our town. Big on hospitality and ideas, most of our work centered on food, generously seasoned with laughter—especially laughter!

This time we planned to take around ten families from various countries across Asia and the Middle East to a Christian camp in the beautiful countryside nearby. We thought it would be a nice day out for them and a chance for us to connect. With any luck some might even agree to stay and hear the speaker in the evening who we knew would preach the Gospel and pray for healing.

Honestly, at the time I thought it was a great idea, and I was willing to support it wholeheartedly, but I also assumed that my involvement would be minimal, stirring a pot, perhaps. It was early in my journey of cross-cultural involvement, and I felt completely out of my depth. I thought I would occupy the edges, staying in my comfort zone. The Lord had other ideas! It started with me needing to use my car to bring a carful to the site. Simple enough, but, oh boy, that really pushed my comfort zone. Later I could hear the Lord chuckling about how He positioned me perfectly to be involved right in the center of things and nowhere near the edge.

But back to the curry and rice for these families. It turned out, of course, they were all absolute specialists in curry and especially how to cook rice.

This was news to us, but it turns out that rice needs washing— *a lot* of washing. All the women from different countries agreed, and as you can imagine, they were not planning to sit back and be served by us, especially as our rice experience in the culinary department was clearly lacking. These lovely women were far too polite to laugh too loudly, but their knowing smiles and chuckles spoke volumes.

The women just took over—not our plan at all! We ended up supplying the water (a lot) by carrying buckets so they could do the technical stuff of washing and rinsing. We all stood by somewhat helplessly while these beautiful women got on doing the work. Don't misunderstand me; they were very polite about it but also very firm. And who were we to argue? I certainly wasn't going to. It was actually very beautiful to see these women laughing, enjoying being able to work together as a community of women from multiple nations, and seemingly managing the lack of much common language with ease because they all knew (unlike us) exactly what to do and were completely united in their amusement over our efforts.

Then it turned out the best rice needs soaking after washing (who knew this—certainly not me), and they gently but firmly stopped us from jumping back in to start cooking. What could we do but start boiling water for tea, something we felt as a group of English women that we could do competently. They did let us do that, though to mixed reviews. Cue more laughter and significantly more sugar and milk than we had bargained for.

I think by now we were all somewhat nervous about how the rest of the curry cooking plan would go. Would we be allowed to carry on as planned? Seemingly not! And of course, now we were being supervised. We started off, and actually they didn't seem too appalled by our ingredients. At least we had proper spices and not curry powder. But their methods were different. . . . and we let them get on with it. It seemed the best way given the circumstances.

By now the men from all countries were happily and comfortably sitting and chatting that universal language of "football," which seems to rely on very few words apart from *Manchester United*. Soon they got the children involved in some random outdoor game, and much laughter ensued.

What we in our planning had totally misunderstood was how much the women longed to be working together to do something for themselves and us. At that stage in their time in the U.K., there were so many limits on what they were able or allowed to do. We had helped in many ways, but they really missed the independence and dignity they were used to.

In addition, many were missing their extended families back in their home countries. For them to be able to work together as women, even for the day, doing something they could do well while serving us was the real gift for them, and they laughed loudly along with us most of the time. They did allow us to stir occasionally! And I must admit the final product was delicious—much better than our version would have been because of their expertise—but I think it was mostly because of the love and laughter stirred into it and the love and laughter with which it was received and eaten.

In our desire to serve and share the Gospel in gentle, loving, and hospitable ways, we learned that hospitality works both ways, giving and receiving. To our surprise, receiving their hospitality this way, with laughter relaxing it all, enabled future efforts to engage. We held many other small food fests in our various homes in our desire to lead them further along the journey to faith in Jesus. Inevitably we ended up having our best and funniest moments over the kitchen sink. It turned out that we weren't washing our pots correctly either! Cue more laughter. And in my case, I had to allow my badly organized cutlery drawer to be seen in all its chaotic splendor—could I pretend it was an art installation?

Once we recognized how important the community element was, we enjoyed more laughter and humility along the way. We gave so much more to these beautiful families than we realized as we allowed them to serve us, working together as women. And they gave so much to us.

And for my story, I knew (and the Lord knew I knew) that He

had called me to serve cross-culturally out of my own passport country, though at this stage I had no particular country in mind. He knew I needed to be nudged out of my fear and comfort zone to begin to step into His calling in this phase of my life. Laughter played a key part as my teacher over the next few years.

It took a few more years of His gentle nudging and guiding before I ventured abroad. Seven years into that journey, I can only rejoice in His grace and wisdom and laugh joyously as I remember this particular time—somehow so much more significant than I realized at the time. Now I rejoice in the mistakes I make, the lack of neat, round chapatis, and the laughter I share with women who invite me into their homes and lives and teach me so much as they graciously receive me.

Chapter 8

LESSON AT THE WATER PUMP

By Sarah Hilkemann

My teammate and I had been living in Cambodia for nine months when our team leader suggested a home stay. This would get us out of the capital city and immerse us in everyday language, challenging our skills and giving us valuable insights into the ebb and flow of village life.

It sounded intimidating and exhausting, honestly. I wasn't great at the language, but the goal was to finish classroom study at some point, and I knew it could be helpful to be immersed in ordinary conversation with people other than my teachers and the sellers at the local market.

We already had a relationship with a small Cambodian church in the western part of the country, and a young woman our age agreed to let us stay with her for a few days.

We made the long, dusty bus trip from the city to this village area, music blasting amidst the nine hours of jolts and bumps. We finally made it to the village and took a motorcycle ride to the small raised wooden structure our host called home.

"I'm sure you are tired and want to take a shower," the young woman graciously told us. She pointed to the water pump and bucket in front of her home.

My teammate and I looked at each other. We were fine with bucket showers, had done that in the past, but the water pump was located right next to the road that wound its way through the village. Kids on bicycles and men and women on motorcycles heading home from a long day of work rode right past the pump.

We had plenty of clothes packed, so we decided to leave on our travel outfits and just do our best fully clothed. We weren't quite sure what else to do! Surely no one was expecting us to completely strip in such a public place.

The chilly water was refreshing, and our clothes were soon soaked. We quickly had an audience for our bathing session. Neighborhood children gathered to watch these strange tall foreign girls washing up with their clothes on.

The comments and giggles abounded. One girl whispered to her sister, "They only washed their arms and legs and faces." Adults nearby came out of their homes to see what was going on.

It was obvious we were doing something wrong. In that moment I could have laughed along with these new friends and tried to find the humor in what was apparently a gap in our cultural understanding of bathing practices. I could have asked for help and requested clarification about how you are supposed to manage washing at the front water pump.

Instead, I chose the route of shame. *Wow, I must be dumb if I can't figure this out. Everyone is staring and laughing, and I hate being the center of attention.* My thoughts ran wild, and all I wanted to do was hide.

The next day, the story of the strange foreign girls bathing fully clothed was the talk of the village area. Seriously, we heard from friends several villages over that the story had carried all the way to them via the grapevine. They laughed and joked, not in a malicious way, but it compounded my embarrassment.

Our friend and host found a neighbor who had an enclosed outhouse with a water source that we could use for the remaining days of our stay. It wasn't far, just a house or two behind her, accessed by a dirt path. "You must be clean," she said, shaking her head.

Finally, we got up the courage to ask, "How do you normally bathe at the water pump out front?"

She pulled out a sarong, a long strip of brightly colored cloth, and demonstrated how to wrap it around her body, tied at the top under her arms. By using at least one sarong, sometimes two, you could get thoroughly clean while maintaining modesty.

I accepted this new cultural lesson, tucking it away for future use. But I also still humbly and gratefully walked that dirt path to make use of the enclosed bathroom.

We all make mistakes, misunderstand, or mix up instructions as we enter and immerse ourselves in a new culture. These situations can feel embarrassing, especially when we have an audience and laughter ensues.

In that moment when I was sopping wet and not understanding what I was supposed to be doing, I wish I had laughed at myself instead of allowing my mind to wander the road of shame. I mean, isn't the picture of fully clothed women bathing at a water pump in front of the house amusing when you think about it?

Being able to laugh at yourself is a valuable cross-cultural skill. Laughter connects us with other people and replaces the shame or embarrassment of a situation with much-needed joy. Shame can quickly internalize the message that this is who we are—a failure at this overseas life. But when we laugh and let go, we remember that even when we mess up or don't get things exactly right, there is grace. We can ask for help and extend grace when we might be the one with the knowledge or experience and can help out another sister or brother trying to figure things out.

My teammate and I pushed past the initial bumpy start and threw ourselves into our village life experience. We slept on the floor of our friend's simple wooden house under a mosquito net with the music of a wedding ceremony nearby to accompany our dreams. The early morning chanting of the monks over the loudspeaker served as our alarm clock. We walked and prayed down dirt roads, sat and talked with neighbors (most of whom knew of our bathing escapades), and learned new vocabulary words that we added to a notebook so we wouldn't forget them when we got back. Our friends introduced us to Cambodian delicacies we hadn't been brave enough to try in the city, and we made a stop at our favorite restaurant for iced coffee each morning. We worshiped with local believers and asked God to move in new and fresh ways.

My biggest lesson of that home stay, the one I learned from a water pump near the road, was that it is okay to let go and laugh at yourself once in a while.

Chapter 9

FOR THE FIASCO GIRLS

By Sylvie Hom

God delights in doing good to people who don't have their lives together. This is good news if you, like me, are a wild and utter mess.

I spent my first few months overseas getting my hair, my leg, my backpack—anything, really—stuck in bus doors. Sometimes the rest of me was inside the bus, sometimes not. God allowed me the wonderful gifts of consequences and feedback—a brief lambasting by the bus driver and my life flashing before my eyes—to teach me that if I'm going to try squeezing onto a crowded bus, I'd better be *really* sure I fit. But what a gift of grace—after all these years in this bustling metropolis, I'm pleased to report that I still have all my limbs!

At one point, I rode the subway to IKEA to pick up a bookshelf I'd bought. I could have paid money to have it delivered, but—this will become important later—I am very cheap. So I planned to tote the unassembled bookshelf all the way to the office on public transit.

When I went to pick up the flatpack, I realized it was just a little smaller than a door and terribly awkward to carry. I imagined wrangling it down multiple escalators, getting turned back by security, and wrangling it back up. *What's that tiny Asian woman doing?* everyone would think. *Why did she think she could carry a massive flatpack onto the subway? With her little snowman twig arms and her flagrant disregard for social norms?* they'd wonder to themselves. So I decided to protect my dignity and called a taxi instead.

About five minutes later, as the taxi and its dimensions came into view, I remembered something important: Door-sized boxes don't fit in taxis.

It was too late to cancel the ride without lowering my taxi app score (I strive to be a five-star passenger), so I just stood there like a dummy with my giant box as the cab rolled up.

The driver popped out and immediately started hollering at me about how big the box was.

"Yes," I replied with my rudimentary language skills, "very big, I'm very sorry." Cringe, cringe, cringe.

He went on. "Sister, that will not fit in the car! It's too big! It's impossible!"

My brain, roasting in the flames of embarrassment, scrabbled for an escape. "Yes, yes, but subway forbidden. Okay, very big, I understand." I flapped my hands to indicate he was free to leave.

Then he took the box from me. He tried sliding it across the backseat. "Sister! That is too big!"

"Okay, okay, I can go," I said miserably.

But despite my protests—and his own—he would. Not. Give. Up.

He tried angling the box another way. "Sister! It's impossible!" He opened the front passenger door and tried stuffing it in that way. "Impossible!"

Finally, after reclining the passenger seat and smushing the cardboard corners in, he wedged the box far enough in to close the door. We hopped in and away we went. It was dumping rain at my destination, but the cabbie jumped out and wrestled the box out of the car and onto the doorstep, getting drenched in the process. That guy really earned his tip.

Me? I didn't earn success—but God bestowed it on me anyway. I wasn't quite clever enough to transport a bookshelf properly, but God's goodness chased me down and brought me the most determined (if also the most skeptical) cabbie in town.

This wasn't my only humorous transportation adventure as I am not always adept at getting around town.

A few months after moving to the Middle East, I stopped by an expat's moving sale. It seemed like a good idea to finally have enough dishes to eat off of when I accidentally invited eight people over on the same night.

The woman selling her things was not the "cross-cultural worker living off support" type of expat. She was the "buy imported Crate & Barrel dishes and sell them for prices that make me think you don't need the money" type of expat. I am not above feasting on the crumbs that fall from the table, so I messaged her to reserve a thirty-six-piece collection of bowls, glasses, and the like for less than the cost of a date at Applebee's.

As you might have guessed, I have no car. And like I said before, I'm cheap. I hate paying for taxis (unless I need to move an object larger than, say, the inside of a taxi). As I set off on the bus toward this fancy and generous lady's house, I congratulated myself on thinking ahead and bringing things to carry my new dishes in: my rolling briefcase and an over-the-shoulder briefcase.

I don't know why I thought the ideal bag for packing a stack of bowls would be a *briefcase*.

The woman selling the dishes was lovely and, in retrospect, rightly confused about my exit strategy. She gave me a few plastic grocery bags when my enormous collection of dinnerware had the audacity to not fit in a pair of briefcases. Once everything was packed, I thanked her and staggered off.

What seemed at first like a smooth street became a treacherous passage: curbs, speed bumps, cobblestones, and those excellent knobbly yellow panels to guide the visually impaired. *Clink, clink, clink, THUNK, clink, clink, clink.* I winced my way toward the bus station, constantly stopping to readjust the bags and restore blood circulation to my fingers. Visions of cracked cups danced in my head.

Down one escalator. Down another escalator. Along the moving sidewalk. Up an escalator. At some point, I realized I was going to the wrong transit station. But darn it, I had made so much progress in that direction, I couldn't turn around now.

Finally: the last escalator up. I set two plastic bags on the step in front of me and rolled my briefcase onto the step behind me. Sweet, sweet rest.

About halfway up, a man several steps ahead of me asked something. Probably, "Do you need help?" or "Where are you from?" or "Why are you carrying thirty-six pieces of tableware in the least practical way possible?"

As I turned to look up at him, my fingers slipped off the briefcase's handle. I looked behind me and watched in horror as the classic escalator nightmare unfolded.

In a single second, this Convenient People Lifter had become a Perpetual Dish Crusherizer.

CLANK.

...........CLANK.

.....................CLANK.

My bag of glassware tumbled down each step, never getting closer to the bottom—but all the while getting farther and farther from me. People were staring. I froze. Should I run down and grab the briefcase? Yes?! I scrambled down the steps. But—ack—I'd left my two plastic bags on the step ahead of me, rising ever closer to the top of the escalator, ready to spill out and rain ceramic bowl shards down on everyone! *Man, who maybe offered to help, why are you just standing there?!*

I think I must have had one of those mom-Hulk moments because I somehow captured all the bags before and behind me and stepped off the escalator. The not-so-helpful helpful man then helped me carry my bags of (I assumed) glass dust to the wrong bus and bid me adieu. I schlepped everything to the correct bus stop, squished onto a bus, and met my husband at the end of the line.

Once we got home, we opened the bags, ready to assess the damage. But dish after dish . . . everything was intact. Even the shoddily wrapped, nested-four-high, sat-on-their-sides-then-laid-underneath-a-ton-of-other-stuff glasses. I couldn't believe it.

You might be a little less of a disaster than me (for the sake of your local public transit workers, I hope so). But you and I both know we only get by on the grace of God.

May our slapdash attempts to get through the day, combined with the miraculous fact that we actually do, point to the One who delights in working through the weak, giving His children good gifts, and chasing us with His goodness. Even if our leg is stuck in the bus door . . . again.

Chapter 10

"I'LL TAKE 'GAMES YOU PLAY ON A TRAIN' FOR $500, ALEX"

By Lisa Horn

When I first moved to South Africa in 2010, I was serving as the director of orphan programs for a ministry based in Pretoria. One of my first assignments was to travel to northern Zambia and open another orphan center there. Tim and Katrien, two friends from America, came to help me through the process.

We started in Soshanguve, a township just outside of Pretoria, where Tim and Katrien painted an orphan center, held a craft day for the orphans, packed up the van and trailer, and moved me 1,000 miles to Zambia, delivering supplies for a new program to be launched there. After they helped me settle in and spent a day coloring and having treats with the orphans of Mansa, the three of us set off for a well-earned vacation on the beautiful island of Zanzibar off the coast of Tanzania.

With Tim and Katrien having spent a good deal of their travel money on gifts for the orphans and me being a missionary and all, we opted to take the budget-friendly train ($50) rather than fly

($250). Besides, what better way to see the scenic countryside of Tanzania than from the windows of our first-class cabin on the express train from Kapiri Mposhi to Dar Es Salaam? We would leave Zambia at 4:00 P.M. on Wednesday and at noon on Friday would pull into the train station at Dar, bop on over to catch the 4:00 ferry to Zanzibar, and then enjoy the sunset from the rooftop restaurant of our hotel in Stonetown. Piece o'cake.

We barely made it to Kapiri Mposhi by 4:00, having run out of gas out in the African bush. We had bought our train tickets in advance to be sure to get all four beds of a first-class sleeper cabin so we would have it to ourselves. By the time we arrived and found our compartment, there were already two women firmly ensconced in the bottom bunks, their bags spread on the top bunks. Their tickets showed the same cabin number as ours.

We calmly and confidently explained that we had purchased all four beds of this cabin, so clearly this cabin was ours. They refused to leave. We summoned the conductor, sure that he would right the injustice of this situation. He meekly suggested to the ladies that they ought to leave the cabin. When one bellowed, "You're just taking their side because they're white," he left, declaring that it would be up to us to sort it out.

Katrien and Tim staged a sit-down strike in the corridor. Five hours and several emotional meltdowns later, we were still without a cabin. It was now 9:00 at night.

There were two women in our four-bed cabin, and next door were two men in a four-bed cabin. The loud woman was married to one of the men in the cabin next door, but she could not sleep with him because men and women cannot sleep in the same cabin together unless they book the whole cabin. It is not culturally acceptable for the two men and two women to be combined. So they got to keep their whole cabins, even though they didn't pay for them. And we, who had paid for a whole first-class cabin, got bumped to second class.

The conductor oh-so-graciously said we could still have a whole cabin, even though these have six bunks and we only paid for four. Our new cabin was at the other end of the train, next to the pleasant odor and banging door of the toilets. It was also the first door that everybody getting onto the train sees. This door did not lock. Therefore, every hour when the train stopped, our door would be yanked open and we would argue anew that we had paid for the whole cabin. Not understanding English, men would be throwing their bags on our empty bunks and trying to climb in. At 1:00 A.M., 2:00 A.M., 3:00 A.M.

I am allergic to only two things in this world, and they were both happily thriving in that cabin: dust mites and cockroaches. So aside from the hourly cabin disputes, my sneezing, wheezing, and nose blowing kept us all awake. I was also going through my roll of toilet paper at an alarming rate. We were each down to one roll. In Africa, you must bring your own TP as a mandatory travel accessory. By day two we were all exhausted, we all had diarrhea, and TP had become a precious commodity.

Which brings us to the next subject, the toilets. I call them that, but there were no actual toilets, no porcelain thrones to perch upon. Just a hole in the floor where you could see the tracks going by underneath you. You had to straddle it and try to hit the hole. And mind you, this was not a big hole, so you had to squat low. I don't know how to describe this feat, and perhaps I shouldn't try. Remember, we have diarrhea, and we are trying to hit a moving target.

If you have been on a train or seen movies set on a train, you know about the normal sway of a train. There is some slight rocking back and forth, which some people find soothing. The Tazara train tracks, however, were not laid during the height of African technology. Have you seen *The Ghost and the Darkness*? Great flick. Val Kilmer is the brave English chap who comes to finish the railway lines in Africa. He brings in Michael Douglas to kill the lions who are eating his crew. The crew, when they were not being eaten by lions, is busy laying track. Think about it, did you ever see them using a level? My point is, take the normal sway of a train and multiply it exponentially for the Tazara train. It's not really a sway, more like spasmodic jerking.

Squat, sway, aim. Needless to say, not all passengers hit the hole. So this tiny room with a hole in the floor was equipped with a bucket of water to wash the floor down after use. By day two, they were out of water, hence the pleasant aroma of this room and our cabin next door.

I must say, Tim and Katrien were amazingly good sports. Tim was able to take gorgeous photos out the window when he wasn't vomiting out of it. Katrien was able to fall back to sleep after finding a large cockroach nesting in her hair. On day three we awoke with a sense of unease—the train was too quiet, too still. Why hadn't we been awakened every hour by people moving into our cabin? Drats! We were still sitting at the same station we were at the night before. There was an accident on the tracks up ahead, and we would have to wait until it was cleared. Four more hours we sat on those tracks, twelve hours total.

How do you pass the time when you are stuck on a train for fifty-six hours? Here are some fun travel games for the kids to try:

Name That Sickness – Players speculate as to what is causing the vomiting and diarrhea. Malaria, food poisoning, allergy, dengue fever, parasite?

Name the Food Poisoning Item – Once players determine the illness was probably caused by something ingested, players try to guess what it was. Was it the eggs or the chicken, or maybe they didn't boil the water for the coffee or tea? Players take turns experimenting by eliminating different foods on their trip to the dining car and see who gets better first.

Find the Stinky Item in Your Cabin – Players first guess if it is animal, vegetable, or mineral. Then the hunt is on! Players look for forgotten food items left at the bottom of a backpack, old socks, B.O., what IS that smell?

Who Can Make Ten Squares of TP Last the Longest – This one is self-explanatory.

Name the Object Being Shoved in Your Window – At each stop, women would run up to the train with baskets on their head full of food for sale. Players first try to guess what the item is, then decide whether to take the risk. Is this item safer to eat than what the train is serving? Bonus points for guessing pastries as *anything* could be stuffed inside!

Name That Language Being Shouted at You at 2:00 A.M. by the Strange Man Inside Your Cabin – Tanzania has 126 languages to choose from.

As horrible as that train trip was, it wasn't totally miserable! I am glad that I had the experience.

The countryside of Tanzania was beautiful. I loved pulling into all the little villages and watching the children come running barefoot alongside the train, buying fresh fruit from the women in brightly colored fabrics with baskets on their heads, and sitting in the dining car chatting with fascinatingly-accented fellow travelers.

It was an interesting cultural experience, seeing the way that the locals live and travel as this was not a tourist train. It was also interesting to see the change in the people groups as we traveled north—different modes of dress, language, facial features, and customs. Beautiful land, beautiful people.

Plus I can say, I survived the Tazara train! Funny thing, Tim and Katrien never came to volunteer again. . . .

Chapter 11

SHOES

By Charissa Grace Howes

I never imagined that language study would land me in the remote mountains of the Philippines—eight months pregnant trekking up a steep, muddy hill in the dark with a faulty headlamp in drizzly weather, supported by two Filipino men while peeing my pants.

At least I was laughing.

The church gathering in the mountains lasted a little longer than expected—well, for American expectations, anyway. In Filipino time, watching the sun set during a closing prayer causes no concern. But for us time-oriented people, dusk felt dreadful, causing some unholy impatience to simmer. *Lord, let the amen come soon so that we can leave.* By the time the amen was said and the warm goodbyes were had, we knew the adventure that was ahead of us. . . . or so we thought.

We would now be driving back in mountainous terrain at night. (Thankfully, I wasn't the one driving.) This included driving through a river (in which we got stuck earlier) and then down several kilometers of rugged "road"—so bumpy and jarring that I'm confident it turned the breached baby in my womb.

Additionally, we would have to hike a bit because our four-wheel drive had no chance against the lofty, muddy hill that led to our stay—all in the dark.

After a car ride that made my baby a bowling ball playing pinball among my insides (scoring many points with my bladder), I was looking for the nearest "Comfort Room" (bathroom) before starting the hike up the hill. However, I respectfully declined our friendly drunken neighbor's cozy hole in his mysterious jungle backyard. *I'll just wait till we reach the top of the hill,* I naively thought.

Why was I here on a remote mountain in the Philippines with a group of Filipino youth? Because I was in language study and was sent on a language immersion trip—a trip designed to isolate me from the English temptations of the city and my phone. It's what it sounds like: being immersed (or more like, thrown) into an ocean of Tagalog without many lifesavers of your native language around you. It's doggy-paddling in the sea, trying to keep your head above the water.

By the end of it, your brain is so wrung out that while your mouth may have run out of Tagalog, your mind continues dreaming in Tagalog as you sleep. I highly recommend such a trip because I learned many new vocabulary words that will stick with me for the rest of my life, such as *buról*.

Buról is the Tagalog word for "hill." But if you mispronounce it *burol*, it could end up meaning "the wake for a dead person before a funeral." Let's just say I was hoping for the right *burol* that would lead me to our resting spot and not to my demise.

At the foot of the hill, I had my favorite travel shoes strapped on. I love my Teva shoes. The ad for these sandals declares, "Step into comfort. From epic adventures to cozy days at home, we've got you covered." Whether it be rain or shine, through rivers or on mountains, these shoes would keep me grounded. My Tevas stayed true to the ad—until this night. Some adventures are just too epic.

With Tevas strapped on, a headlamp (low in battery) on my head, and pack on my back (yet balanced by my growing belly in the front), we began the hike. Soldiers in the army for the Lord prepared to defeat this *buról*.

Also, it began to drizzle. Yep, we are in the dark at the foot of a muddy hill, and it is now getting wet.

Feeling emboldened to take this hill on, I had barely started my first few steps when I heard, *"Dali, dali! Yung buntis, yung buntis!"* ("Hurry, hurry! The pregnant one, the pregnant one!") I felt two young Filipino men come to my aid on both my sides, supporting my arms so that I wouldn't slip as I waddled up this precarious bluff. Immediately deflating my "soldier of the Lord" pride, I was now being escorted like a *lola* (grandmother) being helped up the stairs—yet, I was *very* thankful for their support.

Another youth, Roland, took the lead in front of me as a guide since his flashlight was brighter than my dimming headlamp. Did I mention it was drizzling? Feet sinking in the muck, zig-zagging our way up, trying not to slip on the stones or fall into the mud, we inched our way up the hill. Everything was so slippery. My Tevas, now caked in sludge, somehow stayed strapped to my feet but slid back so much that my toes were hanging on to the soles of my sandals for their dear life. Instead of my shoes helping me to get to where I was going, my feet were trying desperately to save my cherished Tevas from disappearing into the mud.

I didn't know whether to cry or laugh at this predicament.

Then I looked in front of me: being uphill of me, Roland's feet were my vantage point's focus.

Roland was wearing "slides." A shoe style that involves no straps for the heel but requires simply sliding your feet into one wide strap. As I watched his feet hiking in front of me, trying to follow his footsteps to not lose my own footing, I was astounded at his own commitment to his shoes.

His slides glided so much that the soles of his shoes were no longer on the bottom of his feet. He was walking on the wide straps of his slides, which slid to the bottom of his feet. He was basically traversing in the mud with his shoes on upside-down, practically barefoot. I watched his feet squelching in the mud, unwilling to abandon his useless slides. This pathetic scene was sidesplitting for me because I was trusting *these feet* to guide my next steps. Through my laughter at this comical sight, I suggested that he just take off his shoes since his feet were already drowning in the muck and mire.

He continued to sludge up the hill with his upside-down shoes on his feet. Beautiful are feet that bring good news, right?

At this moment I heard one of the other Americans somewhere around me as he was also ankle-deep in the mud. With every squishy step he would grunt with disgust, "Ugh . . . (squish) ugh . . . (squish) oof . . . (squish) bleh."

The sight of the desperate, upside-down-shoe feet in front of me and the sounds of squishing disgust prompted me to laugh harder—so hard that any control I had over my bladder was now expiring. And this caused me to sob with more laughter. You can assume the cycle that ensued.

My vision, already being distorted by the drizzle, was now being clouded by my tears. *How is this happening? I'm going blind, and I'm going to slip on a rock and roll down this hill because I can't stop laughing. Or maybe I will die from embarrassment because I might accidentally pee on one of these poor young men helping me up this hill . . . or on whoever is downhill from me.*

I knew either way a *burol* was happening. I just didn't know which one.

In tears, I begged Roland to take off his shoes. I pleaded, "You've got to stop walking like that! I'm peeing my pants!" He still didn't surrender his shoes.

These people had just met me. I was here to learn the language and learn about the ministry in this remote village on this mountain in the Philippines. Now I was listening to mother nature's voicemail after I ignored her call earlier with these unfortunate young men now practically carrying me as we sloshed up this questionably steep and more-than-just-muddy hill.

And then I remembered that as we approached the top of the hill there was a river we passed through before our destination. *Praise the Lord who leads us through the waters!* As we waded through the water, I was so thankful to have an opportunity for my clothes to be "rinsed" before having to turn in for the night. I will forever refer to this moment as my *"bundok* baptism" in the Philippines (*bundok* means "mountain"). Through mud and water, I came out as a new language student.

It had been one and a half years of a brutal, muddy hill of language study in the dark—tears, frustration, culture stress, and *many* humiliating moments. And now, despite the heavy mud caked on my shoes, I couldn't recall feeling this light. Not only did I learn how to distinguish "hill" and "burial" in Tagalog—I also learned how to laugh in Tagalog.

After being half-carried up this hill and wetting myself, I can't quite say I was a Proverbs 31 woman clothed with "strength and dignity." However, I can totally resonate with the Proverbs 31 woman who "laughs at the time to come" as I learned a new language of laughter that uplifts one from the muck and mire. My language journey, with the help of my Filipino friends, continued with a pursuit of more laughter, with me eventually learning how to joke with my friends in the language.

I held no more resentment to the earlier closing prayer that landed us in this sticky situation. While our shoes were futile, it was our laughter that carried us and conquered this *buról.*

After finding relief through the river—in every way possible—we made it back to the house. I unstrapped my pathetic Tevas, washed off all layers of mud from them, and retired them outside the house, alongside all the other sandals, boots, slides, flip-flops, and shoes.

Chapter 12

"YES, THANK YOU"

By Phyllis Hunsucker

When you're offered jars of pickles or jam, just say, "Thank you," and take them. That's my advice.

That advice comes from our first winter in Ukraine. We were living in a small town, serving with the youth in a local church. One of the girls in the church came from a nearby village, and around the time of the winter holidays, she invited us to visit her family. We didn't have a good way to get out there, but we located a taxi driver who happened to be from that same village. He could take us and her out to her home, wait around while we visited, and then drive our family back to the city, while our friend stayed on with her family. It would be a splurge, but it would be a treat for our family and hers. We decided to do it.

At the set time we piled into the taxi and headed out. My husband Will and the taxi driver were up front. The friend, our three kids, and I were in the back seat. Even such a seemingly short time ago, car seats were not something people thought of, and many cars didn't have seat belts. Each of us adults in the back sat with a younger child on our laps, with the oldest between us.

I honestly don't remember much of the trip out or the visit. I do remember that it was an amazingly beautiful, very cold, clear day. I love winter weather like that: when there's fresh snow and it's so cold that everything stays bright white without any slush. Our kids were ages one, three, and five then. I had them dressed up in warm clothes, of course, and our two girls were probably in their favorite fancy dresses that they wore all the time. When we got to the house, I'm sure we ate, sang, told stories, listened, laughed, drank tea, and visited with our gracious hosts. . . . and then it was time to go home.

As is normally done in Ukrainian culture, they gave us gifts to take home. When they brought out jars of homemade pickles, jam, and compote (the fruit drink everyone bottles for the winter) for us, all I could think of was how I would balance everything on the way back: three sleepy children and all their things *and* huge glass jars. Those were the years when my hands were always, very literally, full.

The roads were rough, the car was small—you know the kind with just two doors—and I couldn't imagine what to do. So I said, "No, thank you," and tried to explain that we really just didn't go through canned goods very fast. Our hostess mysteriously held up one finger, told me to wait, and ran out into her yard. I wondered what she could be doing, but of course, I waited.

A few minutes later she returned, hands covered with blood,

and asked, "Do you have electric or gas?"

Huh?

"Your stove."

"Oh, yes, gas."

"Good, then you'll be able to finish up the feathers."

What?!?

The next time she came back it was a good bit later. Her hands were clean again, and she had two of the world's freshest chickens ready for me to take. I was floored by her generosity and also a little shocked by how different this was from the grocery stores I was used to or even from the open-air markets. Our whole family thanked her, and we might all have been a little more wide-eyed than usual because of this particular gift.

But there's still more: The driver came back to get us. We loaded back into his taxi with one less person this time since the girl who had invited us was staying for holiday time with her parents, and we flew off over those frozen village roads. It was late now, after our long visit and the extra time it took to butcher the chickens. Of course, the kids all fell asleep right away, piled up on me in the back seat. (Most of my memories of travel during this time period are from underneath a pile of sleeping children.) There were deep drifts of fresh snow along both sides of the narrow road, the stars were extra sparkly, and it seemed like no one else was out that night. The beauty and silence of the nighttime winter wonderland were unbroken.

Suddenly in the bright glare of car headlights, we three who were still awake—my husband, the driver, and I—saw a huge hare running in front of us. The deep, almost tunnel-like snow drifts kept it going right down the center of the road. Our driver sped up. Again, what?!? What could he be thinking? Then—thump—and he was yelling, "I got it!" He skidded the car to a stop, jumped out, and ran off to get his prize. As he called his wife and excitedly told her to get everything ready to make rabbit stew soon, he threw his very fresh meat into the back of the car with me. There I was with three sleeping children, two dead chickens, and now a still-warm hare.

My main thought was, *I should have accepted the pickles.*

When we got home, I put the chickens into the freezer. For some reason our five-year-old insisted they were ostriches and kept talking about the ostriches I had in the freezer up until I used them. Apparently something about the feet sticking out from the bags made him think of ostriches. Later I made soup from them, and then he talked about that ostrich soup. I really didn't know what I was supposed to do with gas and the little hair-like feathers that were still left, but boiling and cleaning worked. They were the skinniest birds I'd ever seen. That was because it was the middle of winter, I guess. Not to mention the fact that they weren't plumped up by whatever the stores do to the meat we usually buy.

The soup turned out delicious. We could probably taste the love, the hospitality, and the laughter of that wintery, dream-like, village night right in it. And I'm sure our taxi driver enjoyed his rabbit stew just as much as we enjoyed our soup.

Chapter 13

A VERY GOOD PROSTITUTE

By Margaret Kepp

India is a country full of color, tradition, and celebration. Being a newbie in this fascinating country, I was eager to learn about the many customs and traditions I was observing. And most of the time I was an eager participant too.

Early on in my first term in India, a new, but good, friend invited me to a ladies' dance party. And it wasn't just any old dance party. This ladies' party happens on one of the days before a wedding. Indian Hindu weddings typically last five (or more!) days, and this dance is an important part of the celebration period. Women get together, dress up in beautiful, ornate clothing and costly jewelry, and dance traditional and modern dances on a stage in front of all the guests. The bride sits up front and watches, and oftentimes she gets henna applied to her hands and feet at this time. These dances can be choreographed and practiced or just done spontaneously.

As I arrived at this new experience, I absolutely loved being a part of such a colorful, beautiful, and festive occasion. My friend had helped me dress up in beautiful Indian clothing, but I looked plain in comparison to all the women at the dance venue. I watched as these women danced gracefully with elegant hand movements and countless twirls. It was very different from what I was used to as an American.

One lady in particular got up on the stage and danced slowly and gracefully to a traditional song. It was clear that she was an extremely talented dancer. After she finished and exited the stage, I thought it would be an excellent language learning opportunity to praise her for her beautiful dancing. I mustered up my courage and walked over to where she was standing. And then I carefully shared with the best pronunciation I could manage, "*Aap bahut acchhi nachne wali hai.*" She offered a controlled smile and nodded her head once toward me, but that was pretty much the extent of the conversation.

While I wished we would have talked more, I was proud I actually walked up to a stranger and congratulated her on her dancing. I had learned as a new language learner that one of the most important things I could do was practice my language out loud with native speakers. And I did it! I walked back to my friend and her family members, and soon my friend pulled me up on the stage. I tried to mimic her dance, though I probably looked more like a chicken flapping its wings than a graceful dancer. But I had so much fun! In any case, I loved this experience and was so thankful to have participated with my friend.

The next day I was with my language teacher, and we were practicing the past tense. As I was telling her the events of the previous day, I also decided to share the exact words that I said to the skilled dancer. As I repeated the phrase I had used, my language teacher's eyes widened and bulged out. She paused and stared at me. Then she asked incredulously, "What did you say?" Her intense eyes didn't leave my face. Startled and confused, I said it again, and she looked absolutely horrified. She started shaking her head no, eyes still bulging out.

I was puzzled at what I said wrong. I thought from my language studies that my sentence construction had been correct. Then my language helper finally told me, "You shouldn't have said this. Actually this sentence construction *is* correct—it means 'You are a very good dancer.' But the word *nachne wali* has a connotation to it. It means the king's dancing girl." Then she slowed down and declared, "You know, his harem." And she looked at me knowingly. Further information revealed that this term also means a prostitute!

Then it clicked. I had just called that woman an offensive name! And not just a prostitute, I called her a very good prostitute! I was mortified. My confusion immediately turned to shame and horror. I honestly don't even remember what my language teacher and I talked about after that. But later on at home, I thought about this incident a bit more. I'm confident the dancer knew what I was trying to say—that she was a good dancer.

But oh my goodness—I had called her a prostitute, and a good one at that!

After this reality set in, I started giggling, and soon after that I was belly-laughing. I called a lady a very good prostitute! I had to admit that this was hysterical. I imagined her and the other ladies gathered around her at the dance party quietly snickering about what I had said after I left them. I imagined her retelling this story to her husband, other family members, neighbors, and friends. I could hear them roaring with laughter as she pronounced that a foreign woman called her a "very good harem girl." I'm sure my blunder brought a bunch of laughter to everyone she told.

This became a favorite story I shared with new people who came to the field and were starting language learning. Many people struggle with pride and fear as they learn language, and showing them it's okay to be a human and make mistakes is freeing. I think of how that woman must have died laughing every time she told someone new about the American woman who called her a "a very good prostitute."

And as funny as it sounds, that brings me joy and laughter too! It's really hilarious. There are so many things that are serious and tense on the field. But the Lord has given us laughter as a gift. It's good and healing for us to find those opportunities to laugh and enjoy life.

While nothing in this story is a direct biblical lesson, I think the Lord was teaching me that making mistakes is a part of life, especially when you are learning a new language and culture. If you expect to be perfect, you will quickly find out that you are not. Some people don't want to practice their language until they've got it right, but you truly can't learn without practicing out loud. Our mistakes and failures in this realm help us to grow and depend upon the Lord. Are we wanting people to see our perfection? Or are we wanting people to see the Perfect One, the Lord Jesus Christ?

Our inadequacies in language and culture can also encourage us to ask our host friends for help. It's humbling because we come to share the Good News of Jesus with others. We desire to do this well to honor our Savior and bring life and light to our friends. Yet we have something to learn as well, and humility is a common result of language and cultural learning. I would even say learning humility is a necessity in serving well.

And just in case you're wondering, I've never again called a woman "a very good prostitute"!

Chapter 14

HOW'S THE BATHROOM?

By Gretchen Ketner

Growing up in a small town in the U.S., I never thought much about it. Only after I moved to the former Soviet Union in the mid-1990s and broadened my experience a great deal did I realize that I had added an unexpected ability to my expanding skill set. Living and working cross-culturally had caused me to become a reviewer of bathrooms.

My childhood home with its tidy toilet, bathtub and shower, and sink, all in one room with carpet—carpet!—did little to prepare me for the variety and adventure that awaited in the wider world. Even my college dorm bathroom with everything in rows–rows of sinks and rows of stalls for toilets and showers–turned out to be an inviting and social kind of place. I had some of my most meaningful conversations with friends over toothpaste in that bathroom.

The bathrooms of Eastern Europe began to open a whole new world of experiences. In my first apartment there, the toilet was in a tiny room all by itself, barely big enough for me to turn around. My mother was convinced that there was no toilet paper available, or if there was, it was of the poorest quality imaginable. I tried to reassure her that everything was fine, toilet paper-wise, but in every care package she sent, valuable space in the box was taken up by rolls of pristine white Charmin (which, I admit, was a welcome change from the brown crepe-paper-y version we typically used at the time).

Beyond my tiny toilet room, out and about in town—this is where my bathroom evaluation skills really began to develop. There was the public toilet in the park: Avoid at all costs; just hold it! There were a couple of local restaurants that my teammates and I sometimes visited: basic but passable. There was the bucking bronco of a toilet on the overnight train: Athletic ability required. I experienced my first "squatty potties" during that first year: everything from sparkling tiles and designated places for your feet to essentially a hole in the floor. Any time I was out with a teammate and someone used public facilities, the inevitable question came: "How's the bathroom?"

When the first McDonald's in Kyiv opened in 1997, I was living about an hour away. My teammates and I traveled to the city and waited in line with dozens of others for a chance to experience the wonder of American fast food. The cheeseburger was tasty, but the real revelation was the bathroom. Here was a public restroom designed according to my Western standards and expectations, and it was free (as long as you purchased some fries or a burger).

What a difference it made to realize that I could spend a day in the big city and know that there was a bathroom out there that I could rely on to be all that I hoped for when the need arose. But even there, in the haven that was the McDonald's bathroom, cultural differences crept in. One of my teammates emerged from a visit commenting that she had noticed shoe prints on the toilet seat. Apparently, some people, accustomed to squatting rather than sitting, adopted their favorite position even in the Western-style "sanctuary" of the McDonald's bathroom!

Six months into the bathroom odyssey of my first year in Ukraine, my team traveled to Switzerland for a conference. After we arrived and settled into our rooms, a group of ten or twelve conference attendees decided to venture into town for lunch. We found a pizza restaurant and prepared to enjoy some Western-style food. I don't remember much about the food that day, but the bathroom experience is imprinted on my mind.

Toward the end of the meal, members of our group began to take their turns to visit the restroom. Each person emerged with a similar reaction: "You have to see that toilet!" My roommate took her turn; when she came out, she said to me, "Just wait till you see what it can do!" By this time my imagination was running wild. What was this toilet capable of? Would it provide entertainment during my visit—music, a show? Would it whisk me away to some exotic foreign land, or maybe even travel through time?

I approached with eagerness and did my business; all seemed normal. Then, when I flushed, I watched in amazement as a small cube automatically emerged from the base of the tank. It fit over the seat, and the seat rotated under it, 360 degrees. A self-cleaning toilet seat! This was almost as good as time travel! None of us had ever seen such a wonder (and I've only seen it once since then). A ten out of ten for the amazing bathroom in Switzerland with its amazingness further highlighted by all that I had seen during the previous six months.

During the three years I lived in Ukraine, I realized that it had become my habit upon exiting a public bathroom to provide my companions with a review of what I had found there. I was like my own very specialized version of TripAdvisor or Yelp ("Clean, Western-style toilet, plenty of paper. 5 stars."). But while these experiences were broadening, they did not fully prepare me for a village in Kyrgyzstan.

I had moved back to the U.S. for training and further studies. After completing a master's degree in Teaching English as a Second Language, I was invited by a colleague from my organization to help with a summer English program. We created a curriculum, recruited a couple of students to go along, and headed off to Central Asia to support long-term workers in their efforts to expand their work into several outlying villages.

We rented an apartment in the city where we stayed on the weekends; during the week we stayed with local families in the villages where we were working. The family I stayed with had the usual small outhouse. I felt prepared for this; hadn't I already mastered squatty potties and public park toilets? However, what I found at the school where our English lessons would take place was a different story.

The village school was relatively new; it was a neat, simple building, designed to evoke images of the yurt that was such a key feature of Kyrgyz culture. Like the other buildings in the village, it did not have indoor plumbing, but there was a spacious outhouse a few steps away. The outhouse, a low cement block building, was divided into the boys' and girls' sides. The "ladies' room" contained three "stalls," which were holes separated from each other by low walls. In addition to the toilet area, there was a fairly large open space where sinks might have been had there been plumbing; here it was just dirt floor.

The teaching team for our village consisted of me and "Lisa," one of the student volunteers from the U.S. For the first day or two, when we had breaks, Lisa and I acted like any normal women we knew; that is, we went to the bathroom together. We tried to act in a normal, casual way as we squatted over our respective holes, just a small wall between us. After a day or two, we realized that when the students went to the outhouse, they went in one at a time. "Going to the bathroom in packs" was apparently not done in this cultural context.

After the first few days, I realized something else about the outhouse: it was cool and dark inside, even on the hottest afternoons. I wasn't the only one who understood this. In the open fields around the school, it was common to see donkeys hanging around, doing whatever donkeys do in their typical days. But not being completely stupid, they had also realized that when the afternoon heat became intolerable, the best place to escape from it was the school outhouse. It was cool, and there was plenty of room for a few donkeys to relax.

I became a bit paranoid about donkeys in the outhouse. Would I meet them there? What would I do if I had to share the outhouse with these notoriously stubborn creatures? Fortunately, it didn't seem to be an issue. Maybe the donkeys could sense when it was time for human bathroom breaks and, being equally nervous about sharing the space, found somewhere else to hang out for a time.

The last day of classes arrived. We had finished our lessons and were preparing to leave. We would catch the public minibus for the hour-long ride back to the city. It was time for one last visit to the outhouse before the trip. Lisa graciously allowed me to go first. I walked into the outhouse, and as my eyes adjusted to the dim light, I realized I was not alone.

Two donkeys were standing in the open area opposite the toilets doing . . . nothing, as far as I could tell. What was the bathroom protocol for this situation? I had no precedent or experience to draw on. Envisioning suddenly-energized donkeys harassing me while I tried to accomplish my task, I put on my best teacher voice and sternly addressed them: "Listen. You stay over there. I'm going to be over here. Don't come over here!" (It only occurred to me later that they probably were not English-speaking donkeys.)

The donkeys stared at me impassively and did not move. I did my business, watching them warily the entire time. Nothing from their side. I finished and edged my way out of the outhouse, still keeping an eye on the unwanted visitors. They probably saw me as an unwanted visitor, I realized. I suppose I should have been grateful that, while not actively welcoming, at least they allowed me to come in. It was Lisa's turn to go in. "I think if you don't bother the donkeys, they won't bother you," I said.

"Kyrgyz village school outhouse—plenty of holes, cool temperatures, calm donkeys. 5 stars."

Chapter 15

TRYING TIMES—ENGAGING A COMMUNITY WHEN NOTHING FITS

By Laurie M.

When my husband and I moved overseas, I was four months pregnant with our first child. We packed up our house, getting rid of quite a lot of belongings and bringing only what we could squeeze into our suitcases. Having been told there would be inexpensive maternity clothes to be found in our new country and not having any idea how radically my body would change in my pregnancy, I listened to colleagues and brought the bare minimum of clothing to get me through the pregnancy. As I reasoned, there were more important things to bring over. I trusted the advice of my colleagues—that I would be able to find clothes. Also, surely in a land of 68 million people, I would be able to find maternity clothes.

Each day in my new country, walking from my apartment to the bus, from the bus to language school, and back again, I began to gain my bearings. I kept my eyes open for baby shops and maternity shops. One day, my husband and I spent the whole afternoon walking from shop to shop, looking for well-priced, nice-looking, comfortable maternity clothes. Clothes were either too small, had a new-to-me way of expanding, or were priced exorbitantly. After about four shops, my husband and I struck out, and I was demoralized.

That evening might have been my cultural adjustment low. With tears over splurged Burger King, the most home-like food we could find, I wallowed in self-pity. How could I make this country my home if I couldn't find the clothes I needed? Did I need to invest in muumuus? Where did all the women around us find maternity clothes that didn't cost an arm and a leg? And how on earth could I find them?

By month seven, it was apparent that my wardrobe wouldn't suffice—I was huge. I had complained a few times over the phone to my mom. She came to my rescue, finding multiple articles of clothing at a few stores. She made sure the clothes were large enough and reasonably priced, and she carefully shipped them to me.

Eventually I received a ticket from the post office inviting me to bring my identification card and retrieve a package. When I recovered the box from the post office and opened it at home, it was clear that my mom believed my words of how huge I had become. She had no way of knowing that my descriptions had perhaps been a bit of an exaggeration. The pants she sent looked to be the size of a circus tent. With the sewing skills I had at the time, there was no subtle way to make do.

Determined to fix the situation, I resolved to take the pants to the local seamstress for alterations, conveniently up the street from our apartment on a corner I passed multiple times a day.

Before I set out, I spent one whole afternoon anticipating anything I might need to say to the tailor. I looked up the words in the dictionary and practiced my script in my barely-present new language:

"Hello! Could you please alter these pants? They are too loose; please make them smaller. May I try them on? Okay! How much will this cost? When will they be ready? No, that's too short. That's too long. That's just right. Thank you! Have a good day!"

The following day, with my script and pants in my shoulder bag, I waddled off to the tailor. I was relieved when I arrived to see that the tailor was open and that there were not just one but two ladies ready to welcome me. I said hello and took in the sewing machine, the plastic stools, the kettle for tea, the bolts of fabric, and the changing area in the back corner.

Determined to overcome my anxiety about using this new-to-me language, I dove right in—using my practiced script about the pants. At first the ladies listened with pleasant smiles on their faces. A sentence in, the ladies interrupted with a flurry of words and hand motions. I nodded, smiled, and not to be deterred, began my script again. They waved their hands more frantically and chatted more loudly. They perhaps didn't realize they were off script. It hadn't occurred to me to practice listening to what someone else might say, and I couldn't understand anything they were saying. I responded with a confident string of yes, okay, and thank you—so grateful for their enthusiasm and the work of my language teacher.

Their flurry of unintelligible words continued, and I hid behind my charming American smile. Having decided that surely they understood, I allowed context and experience to lead me as I walked past the ladies to the back corner where the mirror and hanging fabric were set up as a makeshift changing room. There, I unsuccessfully tried to narrow the gap between the curtains to anything less than six inches.

Desperately hoping the world couldn't see me through the large storefront window and the gaping hole in the curtains, I quickly changed into the new pants, securing my shirt in my bra so that my hands would be free to keep the pants from falling.

The ladies continued to chatter away and make bold gestures with their hands. They invited me to sit on a plastic stool and sip on some tea. Not sure that the stool would hold my weight, I smiled and declined. In an effort to connect a bit with them, I opted to keep talking about what I knew. Wasn't this exactly what our language coaches had encouraged? Getting out in the community, connecting with people, and building relationships as we learned to use their language?

I told the ladies I was seven months pregnant, that the baby was a girl, and that she would be arriving in June. I knew that script and desperately wanted to fill the awkward communication gap between us. I also desperately wanted to be able to prove to myself that as a Western woman in a conservative country, I had finally been able to find an inroad to the community. What a gift!

After a few more awkward moments of me smiling and nodding at the ladies' chatter and declining a few more cups of tea, I noticed through the window an older lady scampering towards us down the two-hundred-plus stairs across the street as quickly as she dared with yellow plastic slippers on her feet and a measuring tape around her shoulders. She breathlessly flung herself through the door as the two ladies stopped their flurry of words and as I bore my humongous belly to the watching world.

The older woman greeted me between breaths. She apologized for the delay. Then, in her broken English, she managed to tell me that she would be happy to adjust the size of my pants. She put pins in the waistband and pinned the hem of the pants. I was elated to be one step closer to getting pants that fit my growing body. I could not wait to go home and tell my husband of my successful trip and my language breakthrough.

Much to my chagrin, she continued, explaining what I can only guess the two younger ladies had been trying in vain to communicate to me. I have never felt more mortified as I did in that moment. I wanted the earth to swallow me whole. But even if I were to relocate, I knew the conservative community would never forget this seven-months pregnant woman who had brought humongous pants to be altered and bore her large belly for the world to see.

She asked me, when I came to retrieve the pants next week, would I be so kind as to meet her at her alterations shop next door and not the formal wedding dress shop that we were standing in!

Chapter 16

TALES FROM A SQUATTY POTTY

By Emmy Lopez

The year was 2008, and the season was a bitter cold one in the unheated, dingy bathroom of a hospital in Kabul, Afghanistan. I had just seen the doctor and described my symptoms, which went surprisingly well considering only one month had passed since my arrival to the country. I had a urinary tract infection, a diagnosis that required a urine sample. The nurse handed me the tiniest, most laughable specimen collection cup I have ever seen, then pointed me towards the ladies' room.

I flung open the stall door and beheld what I had only heard from the lore of legends: the notorious squatty potty. Asians love them; Westerners fear them. Quickly surveying the tiny space, I tried not to take in too much for fear of completely psyching myself out before even starting my first attempt on the legendary latrine. With the stall handle in one hand and my shot glass-sized urine cup in the other, I girded my loins and whispered, "Girl, you got this."

TALES FROM A SQUATTY POTTY

I did not "got this."

The first battle was with my head scarf. Recognizing that my shifty head covering could quite easily fall into the mystery moisture lingering on the floor, I quadruple-wrapped it around my neck in hopes of keeping it dry. The second battle ensued as I struggled to straddle the squatty while pulling down my jeans. Getting them down far enough to expose the essentials, yet out of the pee splash zone was a much bigger fight than I had anticipated. I failed to realize that amidst the struggle with my pants, the corner of my scarf had worked its way down my side and hip, thus perfectly positioning itself in the squatty basin for a direct hit from rogue urine.

"Ok, just relax. Relax and let it flow," I told myself. It was at this exact moment that I realized for the first time how little attention I had ever paid to the trajectory of my urine stream. Despite my expectation that all would fall south in a straight line, what emerged resembled more of a lawn sprinkler situation than my delusion of a tidy stream. I managed to pee everywhere except into that doll-sized teacup, and no garment of clothing was spared. My ardent efforts to safely secure my head scarf, jeans, top, and coat were entirely futile. Damp and exasperated, I told myself that I could just dry things up with some toilet paper, then drink some water, and try again in fifteen minutes. No problem.

It was a problem.

The thing about squatty potties in Afghanistan is that they do not usually have an accompanying roll of toilet paper within ten feet. Perhaps because of the damp nature of Asian bathrooms or just the fact that most folks prefer to clean themselves with water, toilet paper is not generally a staple in such spaces. This was when the panic started. I could handle the cold bathroom, the cruel joke of a specimen cup, and the contorting of my body to pee in a squatting position. But NO TOILET PAPER?!

Now beginning to question if there was actually any good in the world, I freaked out a little. There was very likely a small pitcher of water within arm's reach, but in my ignorance, I had no idea that such a container was intended to be used for rinsing down my nether regions. In my forlorn realization that toilet paper was nowhere to be found, I looked down at my already-desecrated headscarf and put it to work for yet another dishonorable deed.

I left the bathroom looking like I had just come out of a boxing ring, but the moisture clinging to my jeans, top, headscarf, and coat was definitely not sweat. I found my husband and told him to stay a few feet away lest he be assaulted by the pungency of my squatty potty failure.

After chugging a bottle of water, I went back in and tried again. This time, I was armed and ready with a fistful of tissues and a more accurate game-plan of where to position the pee cup. While the second attempt was not exactly a lesson in precision, I got what I needed and was able to hand over a respectable urine sample to the lab.

Fast-forward sixteen years, and I still had not learned an important lesson: Squatty potties should only be used with squat-ready clothing. I was at the home of my dear Pakistani friends and headed into their bathroom after consuming far too much tea for one evening. I looked down and realized that my very baggy cotton pants were going to be a problem. The pant legs were long and wide, so I hiked them up before pulling down the waistband so as to keep things from getting too close to the splash zone. Squatting with one arm fully wrapped around the crotch of my pants while trying desperately to stretch them upward and away from the damp surface below, I had the all-clear.

After emptying my bladder, I used my right hand to grab the little plastic pitcher of water to clean myself up. I finagled my left hand to freedom, leaving the arduous labor of holding up my pant legs and waistband to my quivering left elbow. Beginning to feel a little lightheaded, I knew I needed to expedite this process lest my friends find me passed out and pantless in their bathroom. With my pants and arms contorted, the spout of the water pitcher could not access my contamination zone. I needed to improvise, and I needed to do it quickly.

With my left elbow stretching my waistband out in front of me like a bow and arrow, I was able to pour some water into my left hand. But that left hand, the unsung hero of bathroom dirty work all throughout the Muslim world, could not quite reach its target. Now in a state of desperation, I decided to turn my left hand into a propeller of sorts. Flinging the water upwards with all the force that my quaking limb could muster, I got the job done(ish).

Toilet problems are no joke. Tales from the latrine are quite entertaining, and we overseas workers tend to have the very best bathroom bloopers. We also tend to be the group of people most likely to talk about them at a dinner party, and I love that about us. Along with learning a new language and culture, many of us must also learn new methods of health and hygiene. Bathrooms around the world have their own sets of dialects, nuances, and quirks. And yet we do not usually have the same level of guidance for navigating toilet routines as we do for language learning. We literally stumble and struggle trying to learn a different way of carrying out some of the most basic human functions in the world: urinating and defecating.

If you are a new worker, find a trusted friend or more seasoned worker to explain how to use a toilet that may feel foreign and strange. If you are a seasoned worker, get comfortable explaining the basics of how to use the bathroom to people who may feel too timid to ask how to do it. Together, we can not only avoid peeing on ourselves, but also make it out of the bathroom as dry victors with more legendary stories to tell!

REAL SUPERMARKET MOMENTS:
IN THE PAPER GOODS AISLE...

Chapter 17

HUMILITY THROUGH CULTURAL MISHAPS AND HUMOR

By Karis Malone

The sun was setting in the Isaan village in northeast Thailand where I lived with my family. It was normal for families to come around uninvited, and on this particular day a new mother with her baby came over to see my Isaan mother-in-law. At that point, I was quite confident in the Thai language and wanted to show off what I knew. I had passed the shy, timid stage of being afraid of saying the wrong thing and was starting to feel proud of where I was regarding language.

As I walked over to the Isaan woman, I looked down at the beautiful baby in her arms. I wanted to encourage and compliment her and, in the meantime, build a relationship with her. My husband and I were very intent on building relationships and showing God's love through our lifestyle, rather than preaching to people. With this in mind, I told her that her baby was *suay maak!* which in Thai means "very beautiful."

She looked confused and almost offended, and soon after that, she left the house. I still had no idea of the situation and walked away feeling proud of myself. *That's how you do it*, I thought, *giving compliments as a stepping stone to build relationships!* At the time, we had a Thai friend visiting. She was there when I complimented the woman's baby, and she felt it best to tell me the truth of why the woman didn't seem to take the compliment very well. I was reminded that the word *suay* when said in the wrong tone means "bad luck," and as I'd said, *"suay maak,"* in a monotone, not in a rising tone like I should've, I'd told the mother that her baby brought *very* bad luck.

To make matters worse, I'd been starting a young mother's ministry in the village and had been casually educating people on the importance of empowering young mothers. Needless to say, I was very embarrassed and returned to the humble language-learning state I was in when I first started to learn Thai.

A little further along in my language learning journey, I was participating in an Isaan house church. I was one of the only foreigners (except for an American woman who had been in Thailand much longer than I had and whom I looked up to very much). The rest of the people in the group were Thai/Isaan youth, and there were a few elderly Isaan women. My husband's aunt, who is also Isaan, was there.

Both my husband's aunt and the American were women who had previously complimented me on my fitting into Thai culture, so I was in high-confidence mode again and wanted to share in the Thai language. I also wanted to share in a way that was culturally understandable for Thai, and especially Isaan, people. We were discussing the story of Jesus being like the Good Shepherd, and I was thinking about how I could share my part in a way that didn't use the words *sheep* and *shepherd*, considering sheep are very rare in Thailand and most Isaan people have never seen one in real life. As buffaloes are very common animals in Isaan, I decided to talk about the fact that instead of sheep, we are like buffaloes, and Jesus is the one taking care of us.

After I spoke very confidently and with pride that I'd worked out a way to share the story Isaan-style, I noticed confusion and offense on people's faces. An awful feeling came over me as I sat deep in thought, unable to focus on what anyone else was sharing, wondering if I'd said anything wrong. After a few minutes, it dawned on me. I remembered that in Thailand, calling someone a buffalo is the most offensive term you can use. It compares to calling someone a dog or even comparing someone to a toilet. You can't get worse than buffalo!

I wanted the ground to swallow me up right then and there. But it gets even more embarrassing. As there were elderly women in the group and I was a young woman in my early twenties, I had broken one of the most important cultural values, which is to treat elders with utmost respect. I had pointed to everyone in the group, including the elderly women, and said, "We are like buffaloes!" It was the worst possible thing I could say. My husband's aunt and the American woman who had previously complimented me must've been thinking, *Oh dear, Karis still has a LONG way to go!*

One of the most important lessons I learned in my early years of speaking the local language was how important it is to stay humble. Although I felt embarrassed and even condemned myself for these mistakes (and there were many more!), they kept me humble. I realized throughout the years that whenever I got carried away drowning in my own pride, God loved me enough to lift me out of my pride through these embarrassing times.

While confidence is a good thing to have, the times I made these mistakes—and other ones too—were times when I was so deep in confidence and pride that I stepped out before asking my Daddy God what I should do. When I shared that we are like buffaloes, instead of asking God how He wanted me to share, I jumped out with my own opinions. My thoughts went something along the lines of *I know exactly what I can say! I know this culture now. I know what will speak to their hearts!* There was a lot of I, I, and I. Me, me, and me. There wasn't much of *God, what do you think I should say?*

Now, these stories are funny to me. I'm so thankful for them! I love having some ways to make people laugh, especially those still new to learning a language, to relate to them and help them see that making mistakes is normal. And, again, I'm very thankful that God loves me enough to allow me to step down from my pride *before* it destroys me. That said, in the moment, I felt very differently.

By the end of my time in Isaan, I had picked up a bit of the local Isaan language. Isaan is a mix between Thai and Laotian, and

I'd picked up some words when listening to my Isaan husband speak with his family and friends. One day I was at a 7-Eleven buying snacks. I came to a counter where a woman was serving customers. Next to her, a man had just finished serving another customer. I overheard him say in Isaan to the woman server as he looked at me, "Go ahead and serve my girlfriend—she's waiting." The woman laughed, but I boiled with anger as I realized I was the subject of his joke; I was his tool in showing off to the people around him. I couldn't resist responding, but I managed to calm myself enough to stay culturally acceptable. I blurted out, in a mix of Thai and the local Isaan language, "I'm not your girlfriend, and my husband is sitting in the car outside. Would you like to meet him?"

The man's jaw fell open, and he immediately turned as red as a tanned-skin person can turn as he realized that I understood everything he said. All my cultural frustrations from the last year must've come out on that guy through a simple sentence. At least I'd finally worked out a culturally acceptable way to respond, even if this time it was to unleash my frustrations in a fun and cheeky way.

This happened almost ten years after moving to Thailand. Adapting to a culture takes a lot of time, patience, and ability to laugh at your mistakes. I'm still waiting on news that the woman whose baby was called "bad luck" by the cross-cultural worker is now a believer or that the unbelievers in the house church were able to forgive the woman who called them buffaloes, or even that the man in 7-Eleven was somehow drawn to God through a cheeky response in the local language. Until then, I know and trust that God is bigger than what we say or do and that He can turn any situation into good for His glory.

Chapter 18

THE UNWANTED GUEST

By MaDonna Maurer

We love having company. There was a time when we had a family of seven stay with us for a week. Did I mention we are a family of five and our middle child has a developmental disability? But this story is not about that time. This story is about the time that my husband was traveling and my oldest was away at college. It was just me and the two girls.

We lived in a small city on the coast, known for visitors passing through during vacation. During one vacation, some friends called and wanted to eat with us. I didn't know these friends that well. I had eaten at their house once with just my youngest daughter. That experience was what most people would call a typical gathering. But eating out with our middle child is like one of those gum machines that you put a coin in and turn the knob to get a prize. You don't get to choose the prize; you get whatever comes out. It could be a sweet and fun experience, or it could be sour and chaotic. Anytime we go out, the goal is to keep her content in hopes that we get the sweet and fun girl.

We had an hour before our friends were to pick us up. My younger daughter does what typical teenage girls do to get ready to go out. With my older daughter content to play with her Duplos, I decide to water the plants.

I fill my gray watering can and begin my task. Two plants sit like queens on top of matching white, six-foot-tall bookshelves that house no books. The shelves offer space for a few ceramic teapots from dear friends, photos of the family, and other things my younger self would find annoying to dust, but since I have a daughter who likes to dust, it is okay. I pull the first green leafy plant down and notice a hole in the dirt about the size of a golf ball.

That's weird.

I put it back without watering it and pull down the second plant. It has the same golf ball-sized hole. I set the plant back in its place. There is a mystery that I need to solve.

I look at the clock. I have forty-five minutes to solve it.

I grab a stool and the heavy-duty flashlight. You know, the one that has the long handle. I climb up to inspect the top shelf. Dirt is scattered all over the place. Plus, a red crayon is in the middle of it.

Why and how did my daughter get that up there?

I grab my phone and search, "What causes holes in the dirt of houseplants?" Maybe you already know this, but I did not. Rodents hide their food and treasures in the dirt of houseplants.

At this point, I might have a rodent in the house, but there is no hard evidence. Remembering that I have guests coming, I recheck the clock. Thirty minutes.

At this point, my daughter playing on the floor with her Duplos has moved to a different spot, and the youngest is in the room with us and caught up with all that I've found so far. I take all the breakable things off the shelves. I move one of the shelves out just a little. Not only do I see traces of a mouse—poo—but I also see the tail of said mouse zip under the TV stand.

I scream.

My youngest screams.

My older daughter laughs until she realizes her Duplos are near the crime scene. I've never seen her clean up so fast.

I move the TV to a safer area and tell the girls to go to another room. I'm calling for help. I open the door to let in our rodent-killing canine, Marley. She is part Labrador and part Taiwan mountain dog, so she is medium-sized. She follows the trail to the back of the TV stand and sniffs the crime scene. By this time I have a broom ready to whack the little intruder.

I glance at the clock. We have twenty minutes until the real guests arrive. My middle child sits in the rocking chair in her underwear with a pair of new shorts in her hand. Apparently, in all the chaos, she had an accident and is changing clothes, but she is not about to miss the action. My youngest does not want to miss it either. She has the best seat in the house, standing on the chair.

"Umm, Mom, what if Marley catches it? Then what?" my

youngest asks.

Too late for that now. This battle is on.

Armed and ready, I watch Marley sniff and paw at the floor around the TV stand. Then, in slow motion, the mouse I have now named Ralph leaps out. He races in long strides like it is the final stretch to the finish line. I stare in amazement, almost cheering him on. He leaps over my feet and into the kitchen under the American-sized oven that has yet to be installed.

Marley is still by the TV stand. Maybe she is not the genius I thought she was.

I check the clock. Fifteen minutes.

I need mouse traps. I walk to "Everything Store"—you know, those stores in every country that sell everything. I am walking up and down the aisles when my husband calls. I give him the rundown of the evening so far. I'm sure I yell on the phone because I can't find the traps. He slows me down and makes me breathe a bit. I find the traps and go to pay. The cashier smiles at me, knowing that I have a problem. I'm just not sure if she thinks the problem is Ralph or if it is me. Either way, I have the traps and have time to set them before our guests arrive.

Guests. They are NOT coming into the house. That cannot happen.

Just as I turn onto our street, my friends call. They have arrived and are parked. I debate if I should tell them about Ralph or not. As I walk up to their car window with six 8x10-inch frame-size packages with a cartoon rat on the front, I opt to tell them. They nod as if they understand, but the looks on their faces tell me they do not.

I smile and say, "Stay here, and I'll be back with the girls."

Inside the house, my youngest helps me unwrap the packages of sticky frames. Each package has two traps. I place all six traps around the oven like a wall to which we would lay siege. We grab our bags, say a prayer, and walk out of the house.

Dinner is a good distraction. We laugh at other things, and my wild card of a child is the sweet and lovely child we all hoped she would be. They drop us off, and we head into the kitchen, hoping to celebrate a victory. We are met with empty traps.

That night, we pray. I send a text to a friend to pray. I need Ralph to be gone. I hate thinking about his death after naming him, but he started this battle by digging holes in my plants and living in my home. He has to go. He is not a guest that I want in my house. That night, I dream of catching Ralph and all his cousins.

I wake thinking, *Oh please, Lord, let there not be cousins.* Armed with my flashlight, I check the traps. Five traps are empty, but the sixth one is not. I say a prayer of thanksgiving. I am thankful the battle is over, and I did not need to "bop him on the head." The ordeal is over—except for cleaning up and keeping an eye out for cousins.

But none are ever found.

Chapter 19

THE DOG IN THE STORM

By Rachel Matisi

"Please, can we just go home? Everyone is looking."

I'm ashamed to tell you that I was pleading with a dog.

He remained unmoved by my desperation. If anything, he pulled harder in the opposite direction. Someone posted about our standoff in the neighborhood group chat, and people were coming from all directions to watch the show. I resigned myself to once again being the daily dose of entertainment for my neighbors.

But let me go back to the beginning.

When I first moved to Thailand, I came to a pre-established house with my fellow teachers. They'd been living there for a year already, and while they had many great relationships with the Thai people in our church and team, they had been unable to build connections within the neighborhood where we lived. In fact, many of the *farang* (foreigners) who lived in our little neighborhood had found this challenging. Our Thai neighbours greeted us with a polite yet firmly distant friendliness that was hard to break through. I had been there a full year before I saw any change in these relationships, and it all began with the dog in the storm.

I was looking after a friend's dog, Bandit. He was tiny, energetic, and feisty. Things worked best if I took him for a walk early in the morning so he was worn out by the time I left for school. One morning after a particularly bad monsoon storm, Bandit and I set out for our walk, and the neighbors looked at us with concerned eyes. "Be careful," they warned, "a big, black dog came in the night. He might attack."

Bandit and I hurried home without seeing this other dog. It was a week before I saw him. But I could hear him. Each night his howls would echo through the neighborhood, the saddest sound I'd ever heard. The neighbors were divided. Half wanted to put out poison. But the other half listened to those mournful cries, and their hearts broke.

Bandit and I continued our walks until one morning the black dog began to follow us. He stayed behind or on my peripherals, just out of reach, and watched me out of the corner of his eyes. He skittered away whenever I turned toward him—ears back, tail between his legs, his fur matted and clinging to his far too thin body. He came closer again when I turned away.

Bandit was ready to fight, but I decided the best option was to stay calm and get home. The black dog followed until I closed the gate behind me, then with an eerie howl he disappeared under a parked car and slinked away through the shadows. It was a while before I found the courage to go for a walk again.

Eventually, it became clear that Bandit desperately needed a walk. Gathering my courage and praying for safety, we set out, and, once again, the black dog followed, an unsettling presence in the background. He didn't show any signs of aggression. But my heart raced, and my mind conjured all sorts of horrible images.

Every day the black dog would join us for our walk, often meeting us at the gate, and each day my nerves were frayed by the time we got home. He began running beside me as I rode my bike to school, and we fell into an uneasy routine. Whenever I went to or from my house, he was there. And then, one morning, a large dog I hadn't seen before lunged at us from behind his fence. I wasn't in any danger; Bandit didn't even react. But for a moment I was scared, and in that moment the black dog rushed to stand between me and the threat. Hackles raised, teeth bared, he kept between us until I had safely passed.

When we got home, instead of closing the gate behind me, I left it open and put out a bowl of cool water. Cautiously, the black dog came into the yard and lapped up the water, draining the bowl before darting away again. And so it went: The black dog escorted me through my daily routines, and I kept a bowl of water ready for him and the gate open.

Meanwhile, the neighborhood debate raged on, and it was decided that if the "save him" side could get him to eat, no one would try to poison him. If he wasn't hungry, surely he was less likely to attack. Despite how intimidating the black dog looked and sounded, the reality was that he was afraid of everyone and everything. He refused to look directly at anyone, and aside from when he was with me, he spent most of his time hiding.

After a week of trying, a few people had managed to find his hiding place and lure him out with the offer of food. His hunger had overcome his fear. A block away, I happened to walk past that street on my way to visit a friend. The black dog abandoned his chance at food to come bounding down the road and walk with me. I was used to my unsettling guardian and thought little of it, but the news captivated the neighborhood. I came home to a small contingent of neighbors making an unprecedented house call.

"He's your dog," they informed me. "We'll help you to look after him. But you have to keep him here."

I agreed to try. The next time we went for a walk and he came in to drink the water, I simply closed the gate. The black dog was unfazed. Just like that, I had a dog. I wondered what the next morning would bring. The black dog didn't howl that night.

Over the following weeks, Coffee, as a friend named him, gained weight, his coat became glossy, and he lost his wild look. Although he was still afraid of everyone else, his personality was beginning to shine through when he was with me. The neighbors watched his transformation and the bond between us, and my timid storm dog became well-known and loved.

One neighbor cooked dinner for him every night, another went to the wet markets each morning to bring him fresh chicken feet, and the old ladies oohed and aahed over how handsome he was becoming. Snacks for Coffee soon became snacks for me, I'd often find bags hung over the fence with a note and a new fruit or local delicacy for me to try.

Perhaps most entertaining for everyone was that Coffee was dramatic, *very* dramatic. He was not above throwing himself down and wailing, and he communicated his emotions with a collection of howls all with different meanings. If I didn't respond to a particular howl, a neighbor might call out to me, "Rachel, Coffee has something to show you!" I noted with surprise that everyone knew our names.

They also delighted in watching whatever antics Coffee and I got up to. Which brings me back to the battle of wills taking place on the corner and drawing everyone's attention.

Someone's pet rabbits had escaped and multiplied so that, for a time, free-range rabbits were running around the neighborhood. They were the kind of thing Coffee loved to chase, and the kind of thing I wanted him to leave alone. I spotted them a split second before Coffee did and had just enough time to tighten my grip on the leash before he lunged for them.

I tried desperately to pull him toward home, but he refused to come, letting out furious howls and throwing himself after the rabbits, pulling me with him. Coffee was stronger than I was, but I was in charge. He wasn't going to deliberately pull me over, but he *was* going to make life as hard as possible in the hopes of getting what he wanted. I knew I wasn't going anywhere without his cooperation. We were at a stalemate. He growled at me. I growled back. We glared at each other. And the neighbors came.

The neighborhood guard had witnessed the whole thing. He took it upon himself to update each newcomer, gleefully reenacting the struggle, complete with imitations of Coffee's howls and my desperate pleas, much to the delight of the growing crowd. Someone brought a bag of mandarins with them, and before long all sorts of snacks were being passed around. "You need your strength to win," was the laughing comment as people peeled fruit and handed it to me or brought me cups of cold water. Someone helpfully started a timer, and everyone made guesses as to how long we'd be on the corner.

It was Coffee's discomfort with the crowd that saved me. With a huff, he stopped pulling on the lead and leaned against me. I took the cue. Time to go home. I said goodbye to people as we walked, many of them accompanying us part of the way as they returned to their own homes. The laughter and conversations swirled around us, and I smiled. In that moment, in that neighborhood, I belonged.

Chapter 20

A BELLY BUSTER

By Nathalie

Belly buster: *plural belly busters (slang). A very large meal (slang). A loud, exuberant laugh. (Wiktionary)*

In the early morning before the relentless Sahelian sun rose in all of its strength, my husband would give me a moment's peace at home by taking our three-year-old and one-year-old across the dusty road to our neighbor's house where they would wait in a queue for fresh *gateaux*, which are not doughnuts in shape but more like dough "knots."

They'd exchange greetings in French rather than Arabic, as this family was Southern and mainly spoke French. Our toddler daughter would hold out some coins totaling 250 cfa (roughly 50 cents) and in return become the proud owner of ten fresh, hot *gateaux* in a plastic bag so thin, you'd think the caloric contents would burn right through it. Our neighbors had perfected the recipe, and as far as our palettes could perceive, the texture was perfectly fluffy and not overly greasy with peanut oil or gritty from prevalent sand, both problems that plagued many a street doughnut.

When we were feeling especially festive, we'd roll them in sugar and cocoa powder or cinnamon—simply warm and delightful! *Gateaux* are neither decorated with sprinkles nor dressed in frosting, but when I sink my teeth into fried dough of any form, my taste buds transport me back to a favorite childhood ritual: my dad would treat my siblings and me to Dunkin' Donuts on the first and last days of school, and I'd predictably pick one with pink frosting and rainbow sprinkles.

As we continued this gateaux breakfast ritual in our town in the Sahel, I started noticing a belly bloat. We didn't own a full-length mirror, but I observed that my cheek bones were looking more pronounced and my arms slimmer than usual. I puzzled over my belly and found myself staring down at it, sometimes not being able to see my feet. One evening, I noticed movement in my abdomen. Gasp! Wide-eyed and chin to chest, I waited with bated breath, hoping the movement was a figment of my imagination. Yet it happened again! Unmistakably, I saw the distinct movements of second trimester belly rolls.

I instinctively called to my husband with a tone of simultaneous urgency and hesitation: "Hey, my love . . . can you come here?" When he didn't come right away, I added, "I think I'm pregnant." That got his attention! Over the next few minutes, we stared at my belly together. Really? Even after he saw the movement too, he was skeptical, but I persuaded him that there could be no other explanation. In the end, he knelt and held my belly in sacred silence.

Over the following few days, I walked as if I held a secret. When I wrapped a *laffaay* (long fabric worn by women in our region) around my waist and over my head as a scarf, I held my abdomen in disbelief, feeling its different shape, and recalling rare anecdotes of women who were pregnant without knowing it well into their second and even third trimesters. I promptly scheduled an appointment with an OB-GYN in town (who also happened to be the *only* OB-GYN in town). My husband accompanied me for this important medical *rendezvous*. Were we going to be welcoming a third baby?

It was Ramadan, and we arrived a tad too late to the clinic that evening; the doctor had just headed home to break his fast and would return the following morning. This oversight on our part only intensified the suspense.

The following day, the doctor summoned us into his office and examination room. After exchanging greetings and sensing we had exhausted the scope of our conversational Arabic, the doctor asked me in French to describe what I was experiencing. He listened intently, then sanitized his hands and got an ultrasound machine ready. After pressing the wand around my abdomen and studying the images, he pronounced with a slight smile in his eyes that my problem was . . . a whole lot of gas! No baby, just gas. Much to my amazement—and if I'm being honest, much to my embarrassment—I was not pregnant after all.

"I saw movement in my abdomen!" I found myself saying aloud, justifying my pregnancy hunch. The doctor explained that gas can sometimes cause outwardly visible movement. He also said that I was afraid, using the French word *peur* (fear). I mechanically nodded my head, staying true to my typically compliant self, even though I didn't feel afraid. Maybe he was suggesting that I was so afraid of being pregnant again that my fear had become my reality. I'm not sure what he meant; however, a combination of respect for him and his medical degree and my degree of embarrassment overshadowed my need for clarification at that moment.

He proceeded to ask about my diet, and I confessed aloud (with my husband as a third-party witness) that I had been indulging in several street doughnuts every morning, but that my body was shrinking everywhere else. The doctor advised me to cut back on things containing yeast and oil. I was disillusioned. My husband, relieved that I was not pregnant, found the whole gas episode amusing (and I admit, later on so did I), but "perplexed" was my dominating, overarching sentiment in the patient chair and in the days that ensued. Being unexpectedly pregnant would have been better. Nobody wants to have perpetual trapped gas!

Several weeks passed, unlike the stubborn gas. I found myself waning as thin as a crescent moon, a pale complexion completing my lugubrious lunar look. I stood on a wobbly stool in our bathroom to behold with hollow eyes a pair of thin legs and a distended abdomen, the closest I've come to an out-of-body experience. Faithful to follow the doctor's dietary recommendations, I grew concerned and discouraged when I didn't see improvement.

Around this time, my husband developed a prolonged, dry cough that we wanted to get checked as well. We were in rough shape! We decided it was time to seek out the best in-country medical care we could get, and my aunt generously paid for a chartered flight so that we wouldn't have to endure the day-long bus ride to the capital.

On the edge of being underweight, I consulted with a second doctor, who empathetically diagnosed me with a gut health problem, namely irritable bowel syndrome. He advised me accordingly. The start of my belly woes could probably be traced back to a parasitic infection; since then, foods that I previously took for granted now caused a build-up of gas, bloating, and discomfort, sometimes even painful cramping.

Silver linings are hard to find in health struggles. In hindsight, riding this belly-busting emotional roller coaster, which still plagues me from time to time, helped me connect more with my neighbors, some of them women like me with a few young children, our bodies recovering from pregnancy, childbirth, and a perpetual lack of sound sleep.

Lea, Sephora, and I sat on a *birich* (mat) around a *sufra* (serving tray). We squeezed lemon halves into our piping hot *fanaajiil* (small glasses) of *chaahi akhadar* (loose-leaf green tea prepared with a generous amount of sugar). I recounted my recent episode of a suspected pregnancy that turned out to be trapped gas and IBS, standing to show them my bloat and reenacting my embarrassing visit to the doctor.

Like a bursting dam, our boisterous, belly-busting laughter broke through cross-cultural barriers, squeezing out happy tears, ridding us of any unnecessary rigidness and formality, and paving the way for closer friendships—friendships built on the mundane, sacred, serious, amusing, mysterious, and awe-inspiring facets of life.

Chapter 21

REGIFTING ROOSTERS

By Kathleen Pittet

There comes a point in life when the line between the banal and the bizarre blurs and it becomes hard to tell the difference between the two. For example, I had never been seated in a car next to a live rooster before, but now that I found myself in the back of a Land Cruiser with not one but two, I could not decipher whether this was something out of the ordinary or not.

The extra passengers had not been planned. I was nearing the end of a whirlwind tour of several different villages in the province, kindly organized and facilitated by my team leaders and the district chief, with the goal of collecting data about local opinions on potential development in the vernacular language. Our somewhat unconventional group included me, my fiancé (a mechanical engineer), my team leader (a civil engineer), another teammate (medical), and the district chief's brother who, pragmatically, held the same status as his brother and was called "chief" by everyone we visited.

Let us get back to the roosters. We had already visited two villages that day, and our hosts in the second one offered us a meal. We had to decline because of time constraints, but we did accept tea, which we drank on a large, colorful mat beneath a mango tree. It sounds idyllic, but since I am unfortunately allergic to mangos, it was not my favorite spot of the day.

To compensate for not feeding us, the elders insisted that we take two roosters to eat later instead. This was not a small gift as chickens are relatively expensive compared to other meat in the region, and we had no choice but to accept. The one problem was that we were quite far from the church where we had been camping for a couple of weeks, and we were about to leave the next day. Not only would we have to cart the roosters around with us for the rest of the day, but we would also have to find an appropriate way to dispose of them without wasting the generosity of our hosts.

So here I was, sitting on the inward-facing bench of the Land Cruiser across from my fiancé and the doctor with two roosters huddled up under the benches, hobbled by thin cords tied around their legs. Once we arrived at the next village on our route, everyone except the roosters piled out of the vehicle. The windows were cracked open so that our feathered friends would have air and not prematurely meet their ends a few hours ahead of schedule.

Our discussion with the village representatives went well, and this time we decided to stay when they offered us a meal. Now that we had made it this far in good time, we had more margin. Driving on the dirt tracks in the bush is always a bit hit or miss as far as time estimates go. Per the theme of the day, we were served chicken, which was quite good, although we were disturbed during the meal by an enormous ruckus that exploded inside the Land Cruiser and turned out to be the two roosters going at each other. They had managed to get free from their cords and, not aware of the imminent danger and their shared destiny, decided to continue their lives as normal, which meant trying to assert dominance over each other. Despite the noise, no one blinked an eye or made a move to help the poor fowl. Everyone just laughed and watched the two large balls of feathers as they popped up into the windows from time to time.

Eventually we took our leave and started the drive back to our campsite. The day was getting on, and the shadows were lengthening under the twisted trees that packed the countryside around us. The ride was not smooth, and while the roosters did not cause too much trouble, we had to keep an eye on them now that they were less constrained.

When we rolled into town, it was evening, and the smell of cooking fires was in the air. Our first stop was at the chief's house to drop him off and say goodbye since we would not see him again before heading out the following morning. As one of the recipients of our gift, he had expressed an interest in the white rooster (the other being red). "Don't forget your rooster," said my team leader as the chief climbed down from the front passenger seat. In order to collect it, he came around the vehicle and opened the back doors. Instantly, before any of us had time to blink, both roosters shot out the door and barreled down the street as fast as they could go, squawking fervently and making a break for it. Maybe they had wised up and realized what was about to happen.

I just stared after them, feeling a moment of panic, despite having no particular attachment to either of the birds and already counting on giving them away. The others seemed to be equally immobilized by surprise. My fiancé, however, reacted immediately, not about to be outwitted by a rooster. He bolted out of the Land Cruiser, tearing down the road in his long burgundy *jelabia* robe that made him look like an illustration in a Bible storybook even if he was not wearing the turban at the moment. Having a chicken coop in his yard the year before apparently paid off, and it was only a matter of seconds before he scooped up the roosters by their legs and carried them triumphantly back toward us.

There were several children in the street watching, and they started laughing and clapping. The chief said that they were quite impressed with a foreigner being able to catch chickens so well. I realized that this was another one of those life skills which is quite handy even if I had never thought about it before.

It took only a few minutes to drive back to our campsite where the rest of our team was working on dinner. There was no cell service out in the bush, so we had not called ahead and warned them about the rooster, and even if we had, there would not have been enough time to prepare it literally from scratch. Or would preparing it from scratch start from after it was killed?

Either way, we had a quick emergency meeting about the fate of the second half of our gift. The result was that he would go to one of the church elders to be shared with the rest of the church the next day. If the poor rooster had to go, at least he could be reassured that he would become a source of sustenance for a dozen people.

One of our team members suggested to my fiancé and me that we get a picture with the rooster before we gave it away to commemorate the first gift we received in this town. Since we were hoping to move to this town in the future as a family, such generosity was an encouraging and hopeful gesture of welcome to us and a moment worth remembering. A moment that was maybe banal, maybe bizarre, or maybe just . . . enjoyable. I still cannot decide, but I do know that I will never forget seeing my fiancé chasing a chicken down a dirt road in a long robe. One of those little sparks of joy that adds color to the landscape and makes remote places seem just a little closer and more accessible.

Chapter 22

WHEN BANANAS ALMOST MADE ME CRY

By Michelle Reyes

I deposited my coin into the cart rack and pulled out a slightly-rusted, blue grocery cart with the bright yellow letters *Ka De We* on the side. My husband and I had just moved to Berlin, and this was our first time grocery shopping in our hip little neighborhood on the east side.

My husband and I are foodies. I had lugged a German recipe book with me from the States which weighed as much as a small bowling ball, and I was so excited to start cooking authentic German food. I think, in some small way, we hoped that mastering local German cuisine would fast-track our ability to fit in among our neighbors. Who knows, maybe we could even host barbecues and Sunday dinners with folks we met!

From the moment we entered the store, everything felt familiar and yet different. There were arrows on the ground directing us which way to travel through the store. I missed something on our grocery list, and instead of just turning around, we pushed through the entire store, left through the exit, and then re-entered to get to the correct aisle. My gaze lingered on the labels of green and red jars, searching out the items on my list, struggling to make sense of the packaging. Thankfully, bananas look like bananas in Germany—we could easily check that off our list! We grabbed a bunch and headed toward check out with the rest of our items.

Our grocer was an older lady with gray hair and a frown on her face. But she somehow looked even grumpier when our bunch of bananas slid up to her. She glared at us. Then she crossed her arms and said in German, "I will not scan these."

Of course, my thoughts went straight to worse-case scenarios: *Does she not like Americans? Do we really stand out that much? Is it because we have dark skin?* Then there were other thoughts too: *Don't mess this up. Don't look like the dumb American.*

My husband didn't speak German, so I began translating to him while simultaneously engaging with the German woman. If you've ever been in a situation like this, you know how mentally exhausting it is. I could feel my emotions rising. I was starting to panic, and I was also completely confused as to what was happening, which was also creating a real desire in me to just break down and cry (and I'm not usually a crier!).

My husband and I had just arrived in Germany the day before, and already something so small culturally was feeling insurmountably hard. Our idealistic hopefulness suddenly gave way to our worst fears. If we couldn't even figure out how to navigate a grocery store, how were we ever going to make friends in this city, let alone host meals for them? How would we be able to function in the city at large?

There were clear gaps in our knowledge of the local cultural rules. When you experience challenges abroad, you don't react the same way that you might with challenges at home. When you're "at home," you understand the rules and the system. That is, after all, what culture is. It's an understanding of "the way we do things around here."

When you've lived in a culture your whole life, you just know what those things are. You don't have to question or wonder what is expected. And when something goes wrong, you have a higher emotional capacity to respond calmly and logically. But abroad, when you not only don't know the rules but also barely even understand the cultural language of the rules, it's hard to stay calm. It's like your skin is on fire and your nerves are shouting at you, "Get out of here!" Our response ends up being somewhere between fight, flight, or freeze.

I tried asking our German grocer ten different questions to understand what was happening with the bananas. But she continued to stand there, arms crossed, and refused to touch our grocery item. Worse, the line behind us began to grow. The other customers were becoming impatient, and their quiet grumbles were growing loud and persistent. Generally speaking, Germans value their efficiency and orderliness. And I was starting to feel like my husband and I were sticking out as sore thumbs, harbingers of disorderly shopping habits and backed-up lines.

I became increasingly still, like I was a statue, frozen to the ground. My husband had a worried expression on his face as he glanced over at me. He knew I was shutting down, and to his credit he tried to engage the grocer in English but with little progress.

Eventually, our situation became an almost storewide commotion. Every eye was on us as the store manager came over. He took one look at us and simply pointed to a weighing station in the far corner and said in broken English, "You need to scan your bananas over there." Then he walked away.

Suddenly everything became clear. In the U.S., it's not a requirement to weigh your produce. You don't need to know how much a bunch of bananas weigh. The machine at the checkout can figure that out for you. But in Germany it was a requirement to scan and weigh your produce before checkout. Otherwise, the grocer would not know how much to charge you for your tomatoes or broccoli or pears.

That was the moment I burst out laughing. True tears of relief ran down my face. I thought to myself, *They don't hate us. We're not dumb Americans.* If you've ever lived abroad, you know how palpable the fear of being labeled a dumb American is and the great lengths we go not to be seen in any negative, stereotypical light. But that wasn't the problem in this situation.

This situation had simply become sticky because there was a different set of expectations in this grocery store that we didn't know (and which the grocer had no interest in explaining to us). In all honesty, this situation was just silly. *How in the world had the issue of scanning bananas turned into a storewide commotion?* And yet I had also internally overreacted. The grocer had not been friendly (at least, not in the way we expect friendly customer service in the U.S.), though in a German context how she behaved wouldn't be considered rude either. Nevertheless, I had assumed too much about the situation, and that had made it emotionally harder.

That day, with a long line of German customers stacking up behind us, laughter broke the tension for me. It's what helped me smile instead of cry. And, most importantly, it helped the clouds of confusion and panic clear so that I could shift gears and quickly rush over to the weighing station to scan our bananas, returning to the grocer with a sticker in hand.

I think laughter is something that many of us who have lived cross-culturally understand well. Laughter is a true mark of resilience when our calling leads us to unfamiliar and uncomfortable places. It is our secret language and one of our strongest defenses.

We know that wherever God takes us, we are called to find contentment and strength, including places where we feel out of place. I think that's why God gave us laughter. Laughter is a sign of that contentment, an expression of trust in God's sustaining power.

God is faithful. He never leaves us. He is with us at home and abroad, in places where we feel at home and where all sense of

WHEN BANANAS ALMOST MADE ME CRY

belonging has been stripped from us. Even in times of difficulty when we don't know the rules and we feel like we're disappointing everyone around us, God draws us to Himself. Laughter in a foreign land is a testament to God's faithfulness and reminds us that joy marks the path of resilience and purpose.

More than that, God gives us laughter to heal. As Proverbs 17:22 states, "A joyful heart is good medicine, but a crushed spirit dries up the bones" (ESV). When faced with the struggles of adapting to a new place, laughter keeps us from being crushed by the weight of our challenges.

I could have become really mad that day in the grocery store. I could have become bitter at that female grocer and swore off ever shopping at the store again. I could have let bitterness make me overly critical of the German shopping system and constantly compared it to more "superior" American supermarkets. But I didn't.

I chose joy. I chose to laugh. And ultimately I chose to keep going, emotionally unburdened.

I think about how often I laughed while living in Germany—not at myself but at the situations I found myself in. There were so many situations that were unexpected and confusing with a twist of helplessness. But in being able to laugh, I was able to persevere. I didn't equate my purpose abroad with suffering. Instead, I chose to live out my calling boldly.

There will always be struggles when we live in a place that doesn't feel like home. But the secret to thriving is to tap into our

Chapter 23

FINDING A HOME BY THE BLACK SEA

By Sarah Marie

My closest friend, Dany, and I were adopted into a Turkish family by the matriarch, Cansu. She's a rather large, outspoken, loud, and demanding sort of woman. Something about our plight as foreigners in a strange land, not to mention that we were both unmarried and without our much-needed parents, made her pity us. So she wasted no time in taking her place as our adopted mother with all the benefits and risks of such a situation. A Turkish mother is a force to be reckoned with. They are loving, loyal, and steadfast but also overbearing, over concerned, and a little bit suffocating.

We, of course, were grateful for the invitation into a Turkish family, and so our relationship with Cansu continued to grow over our time in Turkey. This resulted in a couple of visits to her hometown village in the Black Sea region during the Turkish holidays. Cansu had a daughter the same age as Dany and me who also befriended us. Whenever we stayed in their home with them, their interactions always made me smile. Well, that is after we had the realization that shouting was considered normal communication.

One time, Cansu was shouting to her daughter in the next room, and she shouted back at the same volume, "MOM, STOP YELLING!" Another time, Dany and I were sitting in our room in their home when all of a sudden the door burst open and Cansu and her husband came barreling in dancing a local jig to the lively music blaring from their TV set. There was never a dull moment in their home.

This region of Turkey that borders the Black Sea is a lush, green paradise. Green, rolling mountains covered in tea fields slope down to the seashore. All around there is life—hazelnuts, kiwis, figs, grapes, melons, and all kinds of vibrant flowers. It was hazelnut season during our last visit, so as we meandered our way up through the sloping village, we grabbed fresh hazelnuts off the trees and the ground, cracking them open with our teeth and enjoying the snack. The local people are just as vibrant as the scenery around them, overflowing with warmth and hospitality.

Cansu took Dany and me to a neighbor's house one afternoon. A few of the village women had planned a little luncheon next to the sea. They brought out *hamsi ekmek* (cornbread with sardines cooked inside), *karalahanna sarmasi* (black cabbage rolls), *moziak kek* (chocolate/vanilla cake), cucumbers, lamb meat, and, of course, tea in the double-decker pot that marks all hospitable events in Turkey. Dany and I had come dressed in our bathing suits, and as the women gossiped about everything and everyone in their lives, we took a long and invigorating swim in the coolness of the Black Sea. They called us in when the tea was hot, and we ate and laughed together. These women love to laugh. They are vibrant and jovial, teasing each other in ways we would deem offensive, but they simply laugh it off.

As Dany and I were about to walk back to the house to shower off the salty water of the sea, an unexpected event occurred. Another neighbor came by with a thin, gangly, blonde gentleman who looked quite lost and out of place. Of course, it didn't take a rocket scientist to realize that this man certainly was *not* a Turk. The neighbor explained that she had found him walking on the side of the road and that he didn't speak one lick of Turkish. She, of course, picked him up because, like Cansu pitied us, she obviously pitied him in his forlorn state. Her next course of logic was to bring him to the rest of the women, perhaps thinking that maybe if they put their heads together, they could get to the bottom of this situation.

Cansu took charge as usual and started shouting things to the poor man. She waved her hands wildly, asking him all sorts of questions. He had no idea what she was saying and looked to Dany and me, hoping we might speak Russian, which we established was the language he was speaking. Dany knew a few words and tried to make some sense of what he was saying, only to be interrupted by more yelling and demonstration from the women. Since they were getting nowhere in the communication department, these good women switched to the next best thing—food. They filled up a tea glass and a plate full of food and set it in front of him, motioning for him to eat. He was thankful for this, and they breathed a collective sigh of relief. Finally, something had been accomplished.

Dany and I began to slowly communicate with the man through Google Translate, finding out that he had come from Belarus through Georgia and was looking for work in Turkey. He only spoke Russian and apparently didn't have any money. As we were figuring out these details, the Turkish women continually jumped into the conversation.

"Do you have money?" they asked, rubbing their fingers together, "MONEY? How can you not have any money?"

"This is my friend. She drove you here," pointing to the woman who brought him.

The poor, uncomprehending fellow made a motion with his hands.

"Yes! She is fat! He's saying you're fat!" Roaring laughter ensued from the women.

"How did you get here? Did you walk from Russia?!"

"Do you like the food? I made it. Eat it. Here, drink some tea."

He nodded his appreciation.

And so finally, after so much back and forth, it was determined that one of the women would take him to the next town and buy him a bus ticket to a larger city where he could hopefully find some work in the tea fields.

Cansu, Dany, and I made our way back home, Cansu laughing and remarking all the way about how strange that a Russian man would be in Turkey without any money. Dany and I looked at each other with amusement in our eyes. This would be a story for the books. We slipped our arms through Cansu's, reminded that despite all her opinions and outspoken remarks, her heart is as big as the Black Sea.

My time in Turkey has taught me a lot about people. We tend to look at each other and see the differences first, but in spite of barriers like language, culture, religion, or socioeconomic status, we are usually more similar than we are different. We all experience the same kinds of emotions and value many of the same things. Laughter, smiles, and hospitality are universal languages that we are all able to understand and embrace. My roommate and I might have been two young, single women in a foreign country, but we found a home amidst the green tea fields of the Black Sea.

Chapter 24

AN HISS-TERICAL ENCOUNTER

By Renee Wassick

I walked through my new friend's pepper farm to the back corner of the field and stood face to face with what was supposed to be the local washroom—a not-so-sturdy-looking structure, pieces of wood haphazardly nailed together with a steaming zinc roof. I was a little unsure about going inside, but I gathered my courage and took a step forward. I hadn't been living in Ghana for a long time, but I had traveled to rural areas before and wasn't naive to the expectations of village "facilities." This was just a normal part of cross-cultural life, right?

As I took a small step inside, I gazed down into a large, dark hole dug into the ground. Once my eyes focused, I was shocked to see that the ground around and inside the pit was, in fact, moving, crawling with a variety of creepy critters. I thought to myself, *You can do this, Renee, you can do all things through Christ who gives you strength.* I wanted to be brave like Joshua and Caleb as they entered the land filled with giants even though my enemies were microscopic in comparison.

I took a deep breath, stepped a little closer, and a giant green and black snake fell from that zinc roof right in front of my feet! Let me tell you that the Joshua and Caleb in me quickly fled, and I ran back to the house like the newest 100-meter dash Olympic gold medalist.

Now I faced a dilemma: How do I tell my new friend that I don't want to enter her facilities without sounding rude or disrespectful? To be honest, for the first few days when the need arose, I pretended I was walking in the direction of the "shack," but I would sneakily detour to the pepper bushes, pop down behind a plant or a tree in the farm, and then run away when finished (how dignified, I know). I realized that this was not going to be a feasible long-term solution as random children or farmers could show up at any moment and catch me in the wrong place at the wrong time.

My next strategies for the elimination process are perhaps better left unsaid; just know that the creative strategist in me was working overtime. Despite my creative solutions, I realized that I could not go on pretending; I had to come clean. As followers of Jesus, we are called to walk in honesty, are we not? So once again, I gathered my courage, and while we were preparing dinner, of all things, I told my friend that I needed to talk to her about something important. Then I began to narrate the dramatic story of the great snake toilet adventure.

We sat side by side on stools, stirring vats of hot soup and the local balls of carbohydrates. By the end of the story, we were both in tears laughing at not only the absurdity of that actually happening to someone (in particular the snake part) but also how I had tried to find new and exciting ways to do what I needed to do. She replied, "What did Job's friend say? 'At destruction and famine you shall laugh and shall not fear the beasts of the earth.'"

We laughed for days at that story and came up with a great new plan to make the washroom a snake-free zone. The fact that I was able to laugh at myself and share it as a funny story instead of a confrontational accusation or judgment about her home went a long way. Laughter and humor are excellent tools when navigating cross-cultural communication.

The gift of being willing to laugh at myself has been so helpful when living in a place where I admittedly do not know all of the cultural nuances and practices of my community. I am bound to make mistakes. Whether it's buying the wrong ingredients in the market (one time, my teammate asked for rosemary, and the seller quickly disappeared only to return and introduce us to her sister, Rosemary) or explaining the washroom predicament to my friend, I'm sure we have all had cultural mishaps and blunders on our journeys. Many of these types of situations could have the potential to turn into a problem, but in my experience having a good laugh about them not only cools emotions but also deescalates conflict.

Always being respectful of my environment is imperative, but I've learned to remember God's grace for me and my partners.

"God shows his love for us in that while we were still sinners, Christ died for us" (Romans 5:8 ESV). By all means I'm going to make some mistakes along the way, but acknowledging my dependence on Him reminds me that God has forgiven me and loves me in spite of all my faults.

In almost fifteen years of living in Ghana, I have found that a simple smile and a laugh can break down walls and barriers. Whether it's at the post office, the bank, the supermarket, or even the local washroom, my experience is that a positive disposition and some humor not only speeds things along but also opens doors for relationships and deeper conversations. When my friend and I get together, we continue to laugh about that time I came head-to-head with the beast (aka the toilet snake). Laughter brings people together, and it can be the glue that fixes the cracked and broken parts of our relationships.

The book of Ecclesiastes reminds us that there is a time and season for everything. It is intriguing that after a time of weeping there is an intended and intentional time to laugh. The experiences of a well-lived life are not for the faint of heart. There is devastating grief, sadness, frustration, and tears, yet God still promises moments of laughter and joy in the aftermath. These have been the healing times of my life. Looking back at myself and the challenges I have faced, I am able to remember them not only with thanksgiving but also with an almost wild laughter that my God brought me through to the other side.

Section Two

Joy Comes in the Morning

Joy Comes in the Morning

By Laura Bowling

Cross-cultural life lends itself to difficulty and stress and challenges—so much so that we often just assume it's "part of the gig." However, in those moments when a beloved teammate leaves the field, when a medical diagnosis terrifies us, or when we just aren't sure how we'll make it through the day, a little laughter goes a long way in relieving our stress and healing our hearts. Dr. Edward Creagan of the Mayo Clinic states: "If a patient can have a moment of levity in the face of crisis, I think it helps them better cope and better deal with the uncertainties of their problems."[6]

The dinner table was a place of laughter while I was growing up. Whether it was a family dinner to celebrate a birthday or a regular Thursday night, we laughed a lot in our home. But in my mid-twenties I survived a violent crime while serving overseas. Suddenly the mood was somber, and I couldn't summon the energy to make a joke. I was now a "survivor," and my experience had shaken my team and my family to their cores. Yet I needed to laugh; I needed to smile. In the midst of the pain and the uncertainty, there had to be laughter too. I wasn't sure where it was, but I desperately needed some "moments of levity."

Gradually, the laughter returned to my life. And a year later I found myself overseas again, still broken but also healing. And thankfully, life abroad somehow lends itself to multiple humorous stories each week. The "better to laugh than to cry" moments started when some of my luggage didn't arrive with me. And the laughter continued when my roommates and I ventured to a new shopping mall without other teammates.

We found ourselves in a bit of a conundrum as the car I was driving had a wide turning radius that I hadn't quite adjusted to and the car ended up "stuck" while I was attempting to park. I was too close to the cement pole to correctly finish parking without taking off the car's side mirror. And since damaging the car wasn't an option, my roommates got out of the car and lifted and moved it just enough for me to straighten it in the parking spot. I'm certain we caused the people walking by to laugh, but against all odds, the car, and we, survived the adventure without any damage.

Then there was the professional basketball game my roommate and I attended with some of our teammates after randomly meeting a couple of Americans who played on the team. The crowd was small, and we clearly stood out. So it shouldn't have come as a surprise that at halftime we were called onto the court to attempt to make a basket and win a prize (to this day I'm still not sure what the prize was).

The announcer made it clear we were from "the land of basketball" right before both of us missed our shots. Yes, we might be from "the land of basketball," but neither of us claimed to be any good at it. We chose laughter over embarrassment that evening, and it's still one of my most treasured memories.

As my time in that host country came to an end, I helped chaperone the high school choir's ministry trip, and my roommate and I were, once again, forced to choose laughter over tears. Due to a poorly marked exit at a tourist site, we were left behind without any students or other chaperones noticing. Once we determined what had occurred, we couldn't even hear the students on the surrounding streets. And considering how loud they were, we figured they must have been gone for a while.

So instead of wandering the streets of Luxembourg, we walked back to the park above the underground parking garage where the vans were parked. And we sat. And we waited. And we took a picture with the business card all of us had been given in case we got lost. And we waited some more.

Finally, several hours later, two of the other chaperones arrived in a last-ditch effort to find us before the police were called. And if you're wondering why the parking garage wasn't the first place that was searched, it's because my roommate and I weren't great with directions, so no one thought we would be able to actually find our way back to the vans. Needless to say, we laughed about it for weeks and gave the students a hard time for "losing" their chaperones.

In the midst of that long, stressful season of healing, God regularly brought joy to my heart and laughter to my mouth. Somehow, in the midst of the tears, there was laughter, a reminder that there was joy to be found, even in the difficult, broken seasons of life.

So how do we find the joy in the difficult, in the broken? How do we find levity when life is falling apart? I think it starts with acknowledging that laughter is a gift from God—a way for us to physically express emotion, a way to relieve the stress of the moment, a way to help us cope and thrive. In His infinite goodness and grace God gives us the beauty of laughter and humor, the ability to look at a situation and see the crazy and absurd and ridiculousness in the midst of the pain and the suffering and the confusion.

So as you read the stories of laughter in times of difficulty in this section, may you be reminded that "in [His] presence there is fullness of joy" (Psalm 16:11 ESV). And may your own heart find joy as you join along in laughter with the women who found levity in the midst of the stress and strain of cross-cultural life.

Chapter 25

THE FUN CLUB

By Alison Bury

"You are invited to a meeting of The Fun Club. Time: 3:00 this afternoon. Place: Heidi's bedroom." The torn-off note on my end of the collapsable table that served as our desk was written in wonky, seven-year-old handwriting. As soon as I saw it, my eyes brimmed. When was the last time we had done something fun?

"Have you seen this?" I asked my husband, who was sitting on the other end of the table—the neat end. I knew my disorganized piles were driving him crazy, my creativity butting heads with his ordered world.

"Yes," he said, swiveling around. "I've got one too." He held up a copycat of my note, same words, same wonky scrawl.

We smiled at each other.

"I wonder what she's up to?"

Our family of five had been in Peru for just over six months. We'd been warned that the honeymoon period of arriving someplace new would wear off around this time. Our days were a whirlwind of language and culture learning and keeping the kids entertained over the long, three-month summer break. We'd had a relatively smooth entry into our new life until a few weeks before, when Stuart, my husband, had been held up at gunpoint on our street, just a few blocks from our home.

I'll never forget the stomach-dropping feeling of opening the door to his blood-drained face and crazed eyes. The way my heart raced, sweat beaded, and knees buckled even before he opened his mouth to tell me what had happened.

It was a wake-up call—for him, for all of us. We'd been warned countless times about the dangers of pickpockets, taxi drivers, and opportunistic thieves who draw you in, distract you, and then efficiently and smoothly, after getting what they want, leave you reeling, violated, and questioning in a fog of disbelief what just happened.

We'd perhaps been a little too trusting. I'd been holding on to Luke 10:19: "I have given you authority to trample on snakes and scorpions and to overcome all the power of the enemy; nothing will harm you" (NIV). *You promised, Lord; You promised that nothing bad would happen!* My faith had been rocked.

It was not often that we were both feeling a bit down. One of us would pull the other up, and we'd keep going. We'd laugh and joke and find strength in each other. This time was different. We were both down. Trust had been broken: Stu's trust in the people around us, that his friendly way of treating everyone would win out over opportunistic thieves and my trust in God's protection over the family, my belief that we were somehow untouchable.

It was during this time of post-honeymoon blues, when things were not quite like we'd thought they'd be, when we were rocked and rattled, that our seven-year-old's invitation to a meeting in her bedroom landed on our desk. At 3 P.M. Stu and I gathered on the upstairs landing with excited anticipation. Time for fun! Stuck to her closed bedroom door was a note telling us "The Fun Club is here!"

We called our other two children, and together we knocked on the door.

"Welcome! Welcome to the Fun Club!" Heidi opened her arms wide and ushered us into her room. After many months of sleeping on a mattress on the floor, she now had a lovely white framed bed with a romantic, draped mosquito net hanging from the ceiling. We were invited to take a seat on the bed or the floor.

There we were. The five of us.

"So thank you for coming today to the first ever meeting of the Fun Club," said Heidi.

"What do we do at the Fun Club?" asked Daniel, the eldest.

"Well, this club is for us as a family to talk about fun things that we can do together, and then we have to do them," Heidi said. "I have a piece of paper here for each of you, and I want you to write down ideas that you have. We'll put all the ideas together and then choose one to do today." Heidi passed around paper and pens.

Elena, our youngest at age four, bounced on the bed and

giggled. She thought the whole idea was just, well, fun!

So, we racked our brains and came up with all sorts of way-out and wonderful things we could do as a family.

And even while we were just thinking about fun things, I felt something shift. Yes, we needed this. I looked at our kids, their bright, cheeky faces. I looked at Stu, his mouth quirked, his cute dimple showing as he knocked his pen on his lip. His eyes shone with creative glee.

I can't remember all the ideas that were listed, but I do remember that the Fun Club decided to walk to the shops together and buy some doughnuts. The walk down the street felt defiant and brave that day. We were on a mission of fun!

We bought the doughnuts and carried them home. We strung them up outside in our courtyard, and we ate them with our hands behind our backs. We laughed at each other; we laughed together, our noses smudged with sweet cinnamon sugary goodness. And the laughter shifted and shook the stress and the strain, the wonderings, the fear.

Our laughter bounced around the high walls of the courtyard. The giggles rose up and filled the space. And oh, how good it felt to laugh!

Tears welled as I took it all in. I marveled at the simple joy doughnuts on strings could bring. Laughter released and made space inside me to see what was right here, in this moment: us, together. I looked at our little seven-year-old Heidi who somehow knew what we needed to chase away those post-honeymoon blues and realized the strength we could draw from a simple fun time together. What a gift.

We had many more Fun Club meetings over the course of our ten years in Peru. They drew us together as a family and embedded in us the delight of being together, doing together, creating together. We bought an above ground pool and played waterproof Uno on floating animals. We bought chocolate and popcorn and had movie nights. We had dance parties and Lego®-building competitions. We played Pictureka! high up in the Andes while sipping the best hot chocolate in the world, our lips tinged blue from the lack of oxygen. We abseiled off an Inca Empire rock bridge into a freezing river below. The kids rode bikes in the pouring rain along cliff roads with their dad.

Yes, we were robbed a few more times. I came to realize that God never promised that bad things wouldn't happen but that He'd be with us when they did. And He was. Always. Still is.

The Fun Club continues, although we don't necessarily call it that now. Even though two of our children are married, family dinner nights are a must. We played Jenga the other week, and I saw through the laughter that we still need this, these moments of fun. They lift us from stress and strain and our deep existential questions and make space for togetherness and joy.

AT THE SUPERMARKET IN KENYA

GROUND CHILIES SHOULD BE THE SAME THING AS CHILI POWDER, RIGHT?

P.S. NO, IT'S NOT.

Chapter 26

BEAUTIFUL BANWAON

By Lynne Castelijn

Life in this remote village was anything but joyful for many years. The spirits, the evil one lurking and sniggering behind it all, told the people lie after lie.

"Don't laugh at animals, or the spirits will be furious!"

"Don't point at a rainbow. Your fingers will fall off! It's not beautiful; it's petrifying!"

"Don't delight in the wild cadence of a tropical downpour; don't savor the fragrance of rain on hot earth or relish the freshness of the breeze. No! No! Run, hide in your fragile huts! The spirits are angry. They've sent this storm."

"What are you doing? There's no delight in the gentle night noises. Was that an owl? That's it! The spirits are out looking for a soul to eat. Someone will die soon. You should be quivering with fear!"

"Your child is sick, you say? I demand a chicken sacrifice. What? That didn't help. Then you need to sacrifice your pig to me.

I know you only have one. Give it to me. Oh, what? Your child died. Obviously you didn't do it right. It wasn't enough. Maybe your enemy cursed you. You should go seek revenge. Send a killing party over the mountain. Yes, that's it. Now go!"

"What's that? A lush forest with abundant growth, your farm on the hillside bursting with delicious rice, ready to be harvested? The velvet coolness of a shaded jungle vale, spring water bubbling past mossy rocks, laden with natural orchids. Bah! Blind your eyes to it all! There was a certain branch across your path today, wasn't there? You know what that means. Turn around right now! The spirits don't want you on your farm today. Go home. Ignore your painful empty stomach. Snap at your children crying for food. This is your life."

And so it went.

Year after year after year.

The Banwaon indigenous people of Mindanao in the southern Philippines were like so many others. Caught up in pain, fear, anger, revenge, ugliness, death. It was not a happy life.

Fast-track to today.

If you were to visit the Banwaon people today, you would see healthy, clean children. You'd be invited into solid, wooden houses, decorated with flowers grown in old cans or empty bleach bottles.

You'd hear children playing, shouts of laughter. People would smile at you and ask where you're headed.

We weren't the first missionaries here, and none of us told the Banwaon to do these things. Yet we've lived and worked among these beautiful people for more than thirty years. We've cried with them and, yes, laughed with them. We've stood back in awe seeing the vast difference the Gospel has made in their lives as they've listened, responded, accepted, grown, struggled, and then thrived.

One of our favorite stories is of Amay Binaldu, one of the very first Banwaon believers. He listened attentively to the teaching of God's Word from creation right through to the cross. It was clear to him how Satan was indeed the one behind the trickery of the spirits. He also saw and believed that Christ's death on the cross and subsequent resurrection had totally dealt with the sin problem, freeing those who chose to trust this completed work of God's Son.

One day shortly after the preaching of the Gospel, the missionary at the time saw Amay Binaldu with his prize sacrificial rooster under one arm, machete under the other, whistling cheerfully as he headed for the chopping block.

"What are you doing with your rooster, Amay?" the missionary asked.

"Oh, I'm about to kill it for dinner. I don't need it for a sacrifice anymore!"

And off he went, anticipating his tasty meal.

Amay Binaldu was also the one who stood staring at the sky one day after a fabulous tropical storm. A rainbow lit the sky. He couldn't take his eyes off it. He stretched out his hands, all fingers extended.

"Look!" he said, "a beautiful reminder of God's promise never to flood the earth. And I don't have to be afraid of it. In fact, I can *point* at it . . . with every single one of my fingers!"

In our own early years here, still in the throes of language and culture learning, we continued our team's commitment to help with community development projects, specifically clean water. My husband Albert worked with the local men to tap a spring in the jungle and pipe it to a communal water tap.

Up until then, water for cooking and bathing was obtained from the spring via a bamboo "pipe" wedged into a convenient spot, trickling out to the mud below. It was awkward, a distance from the village, and when it rained (we live in a tropical jungle— it rains a lot), the path to the spring was a bog. Not exactly conducive for fetching heavy jugs of water or for bathing one's children. Skin issues like scabies, boils, and rashes, as well as recurring urinary tract infections and kidney stones were constant medical problems we dealt with in those days, largely linked to poor hygiene and not drinking enough clean water.

When the spring was tapped and tanked, the black poly pipe lay like a massive winding snake through the undergrowth to the village. A crowd joined Albert and the other muddy workers, waiting, watching, hoping the water would come through.

Nothing happened. Yet there was a spirit of expectation. Massive black thunder clouds rose on the horizon, building for the regular afternoon deluge. Men leaned on shovels and jokes flew thick and fast. The Banwaon have developed a fabulous sense of humor which ties in rather nicely with my dear husband's frequent, roll-your-eyes "Dad jokes."

Suddenly, a gush of air, a spurt of water, a gasp, and shouts from the crowd. Then a trickle, then a steady stream. Hoorah! Hoorah! The people laughed and slapped each other's shoulders. Albert gave a whoop and grabbed the hose, waving it wildly, laughing along, as the heavens opened and rain pelted.

Mud from the road splashed on our neighbor Yakisan, a wiry man with a wispy beard and an ever-present twinkle in his eye. He leaned down and flicked mud at my husband. It was on! Muuuuud fight! Before you knew it, Yakisan was smearing mud all over Albert's drenched shirt. Albert, grinning widely, picked up Yakisan, marched him over to the biggest mud puddle of all, and plonked him down right in the middle.

The watching crowd went wild, laughing and shouting and slapping at each other.

A bond was formed that day. Through mud, hard work, the promise of clean water, and mutual respect and laughter.

And so it's continued.

As the Banwaon believers have grown and matured in their faith, so has their joy. The truth of their full acceptance in Christ, chosen and beloved by Him, has woven itself into their reality. Their physical lives have improved and so has their perspective. Theirs is a rich, growing enjoyment of life, a heavenly perception, a vibrancy.

I thought about these things recently. We were in the middle of an intense six weeks of recording the newly translated Banwaon

New Testament. The organization Faith Comes by Hearing partnered with us, and day after day, in the intense heat and humidity, for long hours, I'd hear the sounds of the team down in the office working away—recording, checking, rerecording, checking again. It was wonderful work but, yes, incredibly intense.

Yet every day, I'd find myself smiling while listening to intermittent peals of laughter coming from the office. A word said in a funny way. Someone who just couldn't get it and was on their tenth time of trying, only to wobble the phrase yet again. The brave guy who said he'd take the part reading Satan's lines, trying to laugh maliciously as Jesus hangs on the cross but coming across more like a jolly Santa Claus instead—ho, ho, ho.

Oh how they laughed and laughed! We marveled that it was never cruel laughter, the one who'd messed up chortling as much as anyone, just simple sweet humor, seeing the fun in it all.

And as I busied myself making coffees and meals and praying and praying and praying some more, my heart overflowed with gratitude and joy.

The Gospel has indeed made all the difference.

Our hearts soar, and we pinch ourselves that we get to see it firsthand, let alone have a part in all God is doing here. Is it always easy, fun, fabulous? Don't be silly. Of course not. We live in a remote location. There is still poverty. This year alone there has been death, hardship, pain. And yet . . . now we are the ones blessed, learning, ever growing as we see how Christ and His gifts of life, love, joy, beauty, eternity, and hope are very real in the daily lives of the Banwaon believers.

Maybe it's because life here is still raw? Without the "crutches" we typically turn to in our Western culture—our resources, technology, savings, insurance, the government—there's freedom in knowing God is surely the One who will help, heal, deliver. God and God alone. I'm challenged to be more like my Banwaon family in Christ, to look first and foremost to the One who holds all things together.

I'm also challenged to hold lightly the things we cling to or so ardently pursue in our affluent cultures. And when troubled times come, I remember the glorious switch, that chiastic pattern, the way God has of flipping things totally on their head (of which the cross is the primary example), and how He turned the darkness the Banwaon were in to life and joy and yes, laughter.

> *"You have turned my mourning into joyful dancing. You have taken away my clothes of mourning and clothed me with joy, that I might sing praises to you and not be silent. O Lord my God, I will give you thanks forever!"* Psalm 30:11-12 NLT

Chapter 27

TAKE COURAGE!

By Linda Crouch

In January 1991, my husband Jim, principal of a boarding school in Africa, flew to London with other school administrators for a conference. I stayed behind with our five children and prayed for Jim's plans to see a cardiologist while there. He had been having several strange episodes with his heart, and our organization physicians recommended that he have further tests when he traveled to England.

We were thankful for a couple in our organization who could liaise with specialty doctors in other areas. The husband made arrangements for Jim to have tests done following the meetings. It was soon discovered he would need immediate surgery for an aortic heart valve replacement. He would not be able to return home until after the surgery. Doctors recommended that I join him as soon as possible.

I, along with the rest of my teammates, was preparing for our annual conference. I always looked forward to connecting with the other missionaries and playing the piano for our worship sessions. Upon hearing of Jim's upcoming surgery and the need for me to come quickly, I prayed for wisdom as I walked over to see long-time friends whom Jim and I deeply respected. Before I even finished sharing the news, the wife said, "Linda, of course you should go! We will keep all five of your kids, and we will help you to be ready to go tomorrow." What an assurance that God was already in front, preparing the way for my travel and the care for our children so I could support my husband at this critical time.

Upon arrival in England, I was warmly welcomed into the home of the couple helping us, who opened their home to many. Thankfully I was able to be with Jim when he went in for surgery. God "arranged" for a kind African ICU nurse to attend him following the successful surgery. Even in a country far from home, we felt God's loving touch.

Each day I traveled back and forth on the train to the hospital where I would visit Jim who was slowly recovering. The third day complications set in, and Jim needed a triple dose of antibiotics to attack the infection. It was hard to see him cry in pain as the IVs were administered. I made colorful signs with verses that reminded us of God's loving control and help through it all and put them around his room. Every night I returned to our friends' home, a hospitable oasis where I would enjoy sharing dinner with others.

One gray morning a week after surgery, I again boarded the train and began journaling as I had been doing each morning on the commute. The cold, rainy day matched my feelings of fear and dread, wondering how Jim had fared through the night and remembering his deep discouragement the day before. "Lord, thank You that You know what Jim has been going through and the pain that he's experiencing. You know how hard it's been to be optimistic about the journey we're on. I wonder how our kids are doing. I hope they're not a burden to those caring for them. Lord, I need Your help today to encourage Jim, to love him through the pain, and to give him hope. Your Word promises to renew our strength as we depend on You. Thank You for holding us up with your righteous right hand as Isaiah 41:10 says. I'm counting on that strength and help today."

As I continued writing, I casually looked up through the dingy train windows and was shocked to see, scrawled on a huge billboard we were passing at that very instant, two large words: TAKE COURAGE. I couldn't believe the timing of it all. During a usually dull forty-five-minute train ride, I had looked up at the precise moment to see the only possible words that could give me hope for the day! I was beside myself with joy and gratitude. "God," I continued writing, "thank You for giving me Your personal and timely comfort today! Thank You for giving me something fresh to share with Jim. May it remind us of Your presence with us and give us perseverance."

Jim was interested to hear the train-sign story, and both of us felt the uplift of God's love. Returning home that evening, I was eager to share how God had miraculously brought about His personal boost of encouragement that day. Our friend met me at the train station, but I waited till dinner to tell the story. As I relayed it detail by detail and got to the part of seeing the big TAKE COURAGE sign, the couple began to laugh out loud. I was hurt by their seemingly condescending response. Was this another example of me struggling to understand British humor like I had done watching a movie with them earlier?

They soon stopped laughing and calmly said, "Linda, COURAGE is a kind of English beer! They're only encouraging you to drink it!" Then it was my turn to laugh, realizing that once again, God used something for a higher purpose than it was intended! We had seen those same words and "took courage" to trust Him for Jim's full restoration. Jim was in the hospital for two weeks and was back at our friends' comfortable home for two more weeks of recovery. Exactly a month later we returned to Africa and were reunited with family. We were able to share many fresh stories of God's sense of humor and His amazing grace and faithfulness through it all.

Chapter 28

SOGGY BUT STILL SMILING

By Nikki Howell

"I know it's not very convenient, but I am starting to feel nauseated. I'm so hungry." I smiled at my pregnant friend with compassion, her exhausted face mirroring my own. We were both in the first trimester of our pregnancies, her first, my third. "Sure, I'll go downstairs and find us something to eat," I replied as if it were a simple errand.

Slowly I made my way in the darkness down the stairs, my feet becoming immersed in pungent grayish water before I reached the bottom, sending ripples through the lake that formerly was our living room. I waded through the water; my bewildered eyes still unable to fully comprehend my surroundings. Our couch rested on top of our table. Our fridge and washing machine had been hoisted on top of our kitchen countertop. Bookshelves were emptied of their contents; their wooden frames already swollen with water damage.

The rain had stopped, but the water level, already nearing my waist, slowly continued to rise as water flooded into our neighborhood from surrounding roadways and runoffs. I made my way to the kitchen but soon realized that all of the food in our pantry cupboard was blocked by stacked furniture. Then I remembered that I kept tortillas in another cupboard with my spices and made my way back upstairs, rather triumphant with our procured dinner.

"It's not much of a feast, especially considering how much of an appetite we worked up this evening," I admitted to my friend. My husband emerged from the bedroom onto the balcony where we sat in the moonlight, overlooking the river (also known as our street) below.

"We also have the licorice you brought us from Canada," he added with a grin.

And so the three of us—the five of us if you include embryos—supped on plain tortillas and red licorice as our minds replayed the catastrophic events of the day. We had been out of the city, showing our visiting friend some of the tourist sites, and had returned late in the day to massive flooding in our neighborhood, including a foot of dirty water already inside our house. We had frantically moved everything we could up to the second floor, alternating between heavy lifting and keeping my two- and four-year-olds out of the "swimming pool." It wasn't until several hours later that we had realized our hunger.

We solemnly chewed our meager meal when suddenly a chuckle disrupted the silence of the night. I don't remember who started it, but soon the three of us joined in a chorus of laughter. It was just such a funny picture, two pregnant ladies with our absurd ingredients, banqueting on a balcony in the darkness of the night, surrounded by rising floodwaters. Sometimes there's nothing else you can do but laugh! Confident in our relative safety on the second floor, we had opted to spend the night there as the kids were already asleep. We planned to evacuate in the morning.

The following day my father-in-law, who also lived in our city, showed up at our front door in his kayak. Our boys squealed with delight as they were evacuated to higher ground. The water would have been up to my armpits in the street, so I was very thankful to be floating aboard the kayak. I glanced up to see one of my neighbors standing on her balcony and filming the scene on her phone, clearly amused by the unusual sight below. We were among the first to leave, but the city would send in the fire department with their inflatable boat a day or two later to evacuate the remaining residents as well as the sheep who lived on their rooftops. Again, I found myself smiling, despite the lingering shock. "Won't this be a story to tell one day," I mused.

It wasn't all smiles and giggles, however, not by a long shot. Shortly after being evacuated to my in-laws' apartment, a heavy shroud of despondency settled on my shoulders, and tears were only moments away at all times. Later that day around the dinner table, my well-meaning family tried to use some humor to lighten the mood. Instead of joining in, I found myself becoming angry. *How dare they make light of one of the biggest tragedies of my life?* We had left everything to come to live in a foreign land and then had lost our only home.

More than physical loss, we were grappling with the aftershock of feeling unprepared, unsafe, unmoored. I didn't extend grace in that moment to recognize that this was their coping method, honed from decades overseas and countless losses and trauma of their own. I pushed my chair back from the table with a screech. "I'm just not ready to laugh about this yet," I muttered, the words becoming choked with emotion as I turned and fled from the room.

I spent a lot of time in the days that followed face down on the bed, crying and questioning God. I was in the thick of it, and perspective was hard to find. We were only four months away from finishing our two-year apprenticeship and had already navigated several trials, from having a rock thrown through our car window during a political protest, to hospitalization and surgery for our oldest following a scary infection.

I was bone-weary and could have slept for a month. I couldn't imagine finding the strength to sort, clean, replace ruined items, and move it all to a new house. I cringed at the thought of bartering for appliances in the market again. And would I ever get the stench of floodwater out of my furniture? I felt like I had been chewed up and spat out. Not to mention the toll the early months of pregnancy during the hot season were taking on my body and the concern that all this stress was impacting the baby. The last thing I wanted in my hair-trigger, raw emotional state was to "count it all joy."

Yet in the midst of hardship God was weaving the glimmering thread of laughter throughout this story. He was teaching me a new definition of joy, leading me to realize just how flat my former understanding had been. At times this joy was gifted, like the unexpected laughter on the balcony that first night or a trip to the beach with our friend the day before she flew out. I remember praying over our lunch, asking God to both bless the food and to provide us a home in quick succession. Before I said "Amen," I found myself in stitches because of the absurd juxtaposition of a mundane, everyday request beside such a massive, needy plea.

Other times joy was chosen. Like when I created a group chat to coordinate the people helping us move our salvaged belongings out of our house once the waters had receded and named it: "Soggy but Still Smiling." Admittedly, it was more of a resolution than a felt reality. Yet on that day surrounded by the generosity of servant-hearted friends, both expat and local, through the empowerment of the Holy Spirit, we effortlessly embodied that sentiment. Or, as Eugene Peterson more eloquently phrased it: "Immersed in tears, yet always filled with deep joy" (2 Corinthians 6:10 MSG).

And indeed, we had reason for joy. Several days after the flood, after our friend returned to Canada, we began hunting for a new home. God provided us with an apartment right across the street from my in-laws. And God's humorous touch: It was on the fifth floor. Those ninety steps from the ground up to the apartment door were our version of the rainbow from Genesis 9: God's promise that we wouldn't be flooded again! (I will admit I struggled to smile every time I climbed those five flights of stairs with my growing belly.)

Through this experience and other trials that have followed, I've come to see laughter in the midst of sorrow more as a soothing balm and less as a report card for how well I'm weathering the storm. I used to think that those who embraced joy during trials were surely the most formidable of God's servants, their smiles a testimony to their prowess and maturity, proving to those around them—and to God—that they were worthy of their calling.

Instead, I've learned that joy is a divine gift, lavished on us by the One who knows sorrow more intimately than we ever will. Like an unexpected rainbow that appears even while the storm rages on, an outburst of laughter can suddenly manifest in the middle of a crying session, causing sobs and snorts to intertwine in a chorus of worship that is a sweet sound in the Father's ears.

Chapter 29

WHEN JOY FLIES BY

By Natalie Hutchings

At times I find it hard to describe the way it feels living in such an isolated place. Our team moved into this remote village back in 2019. I remember those initial feelings as I sat on my porch and looked out at that view. Mountains, trees, valley systems, and the occasional clearing with a hut or two was all I could see. So vast a valley system!

I would never have called myself a city girl, but even growing up in a small town I knew what it was like to live in a place with a lot of infrastructure and a relatively large population. I did not know what it was like to live in a remote place, and living in the middle of a jungle takes quite a bit of getting used to. Growing up, the view from my childhood home was also beautiful, but in the far distance, about seventy kilometers away, we could see the city of Sydney on the horizon. I really had no idea what it would mean to live in a place surrounded only by nature.

As we press on in learning the language and culture of this

people group, I am continually aware of how isolated we are. The challenge is good for me because I am a people person and have always relied heavily on those dear and comforting relationships with people who know me so well. Being in a place without those many relationships pushes me to a deeper abiding relationship with my Lord Jesus. Yes, we are isolated, but we are certainly not alone!

Our ministry here relies heavily upon aviation partners. We are grateful for the way in which we are supported by our helicopter and lightplane organizations. We simply could not be here without them. It would be so lovely if pilots could pop in for a cuppa from time to time, but we do not have an airstrip in our village, just a place big enough and flat enough for a helicopter to land.

I experience sheer joy when a plane flies by in this remote part of the world and the pilot takes just a little extra time to say hello. You see, something we do, which began almost by default, is to stop everything if a plane flies by. Together with our teammate, we drop everything and run for the helipad. Whether we are in the middle of a language session, in the garden with a friend, or in the middle of homeschool activities, we put everything on hold and embrace the overhead visit.

Nothing beats that bubbling up of emotion when we hear an aircraft approaching. It might be my husband or one of my kids who suddenly shouts, "I hear a plane coming!" If that sound grows louder—and this might only be once every three months—within a moment excitement levels go through the roof, and everyone is scrambling to get to that helipad as fast as possible! Sometimes it means running to grab your shoes. Other times it means remembering to turn off the gas stove before running out the door, and for us ladies it always means grabbing a skirt to throw on over our shorts. A flurry of activity erupts, and even our little dog barks and spins around with excitement.

The pilot circles around to get a little lower, giving us that extra bit of time to run down the trail. The excitement is indescribable, the emotion raw. Our kids do just fine; they can move fast on these jungle trails, but for me it isn't so easy. We also have fences to climb over before we arrive at that helipad. On one occasion, I was videoing the fast and furious excitement, and as I jumped that fence, I only just cleared it! My heart raced, and the laughter and smile left both my belly and face a bit sore.

Once everyone gathers on the helipad, we laugh together with excitement as we watch the plane approaching. Within what seems like seconds the plane is right above us, zooming low overhead and giving us a wave, tipping from side to side. We all, along with our local friends who have learned to enjoy these moments, jump up and down, shout and cheer as the plane continues its journey.

Then, so often, we think back to that first time a plane made a visit like this, and oh how we giggle remembering the confusion it caused and how some ran for safety in the jungle. One of my closest friends here giggles every time I remind her of the time she ran to wave to the plane, and in her excitement completely forgot about her baby sleeping in the string bag back in her garden.

On two occasions now, we have had the extra excitement of an air drop. On both occasions, the small parcel thrown out by the pilot has come with a bright pink string attached. Meters of bright pink drop down into the thick brush! It is such a delight to watch the local kids scrambling for a portion of pink string and finding all sorts of fun ways to play with it.

For the first airdrop, we remembered all the rules the pilot shared with us; safety rule number one is that you don't stand near the drop zone. The second airdrop came about two years later. Oh, how we laughed at ourselves upon receiving a message from the pilot after our second airdrop. "Guys, you weren't supposed to be standing in the drop zone!" Apparently, our exciting practice of running to wave to the plane replaced our memory of the all-important airdrop rule number one.

Finding ways to enjoy life here in the jungle doesn't always come naturally. We battle feelings of isolation, yet we must also dedicate ourselves to language study, grammatical analysis, culture investigation, homeschool, and other daily chores. We are still new to this way of life but have quickly learned to look for and put into practice things that bring us joy, especially if those can be shared with the local people whom the Lord has called us to serve.

Flyby moments have become one of the most joyful experiences of life here. More often than not, these moments come as a total surprise to us, but I know with all my heart that it is never a surprise to the Lord. He knows when those feelings of isolation are zapping our joy. He knows when homesickness is impacting daily life. He knows when too many days have passed by without a good belly laugh.

After the plane has passed by, the excitement has died down, and our friends have returned to their day's activities, we, too, return to what we were doing beforehand. As I walk back along the trail, I find I must catch my breath. As I do, tears of joy fall, and I remember that there are just a few who know exactly where we are in this vast valley system. As soon as that thought comes, so does another. I am reminded ever so gently by the Lord that He, too, of course, knows where I am. The mountains around me can never hide me from His sight. He knows my location, but even more than this, He knows me. He is my joy.

Chapter 30

LUNCH IS NO LAUGHING MATTER

By Anna Brotherson

The most intense and memorable laugh of my life came upon me while I sat on a bed in an up-market hotel in Jakarta, Indonesia. It was Friday, November 22, 2019. If I look back at my calendar for that day, it reads, "Anna and Jo getaway, bring piano stool, lunch, G&T."

That calendar entry pretty much sums it up. First: *Anna and Jo getaway.* I was headed off to Jakarta for one much-anticipated night at a schmick hotel with my dear friend Jo. Originally from England, Jo and her family lived in a quiet beachside town on the island of Sumatra, while my family and I lived in a bustling megacity in the highlands of Java. We had met through our organization's annual field conference, and we hit it off immediately. Our kids (three apiece) were all the same ages and also got along well. All of us—kids and mothers—were perpetually short on friends on the field, and so, from time to time, one of us would pack the kids onto a plane and go visit the other. We sustained our inter-island friendship, between conferences and occasional visits, through long, rambling voice messages sent over Signal.

And so, our night together in a fancy hotel in the capital—kid-free this time—was a bright spot on my calendar.

The next part of the calendar entry read: *bring piano stool*. If you guessed that I'd planned to do a spot of playing on any spare, stool-less piano we found lying around the hotel, you'd be mistaken. It was something else entirely. Two months before this getaway, we'd learned that my husband had been appointed to a job back in Australia, our home country. After more than nine years living in Indonesia, we would be leaving permanently that December.

While there were plenty of things to look forward to about returning to Australia, the decision had brought on waves of deep grief for me. I had spent the past weeks sifting through every item we owned, from the brightly-colored plastic drawer units and the mosquito nets over our beds, to the cups, the towels, the half-used-up suncream—each item, each piece of our life, needed to be shipped, sold, given away, or thrown away.

Jo's son had been learning piano, just like my son, and I remembered that during one of their visits she'd admired our piano stool. It was one of the few attractive pieces of furniture we owned. And so I had decided to give it to her in Jakarta as a farewell gift.

Although it was meaningful to give things away to treasured friends, as I oversaw the gradual disappearance of all our possessions from our home, I increasingly felt bleak and bereft. At the same time, we had a head-spinning schedule of "last goodbyes" planned for everyone we'd known, cared about, and worked alongside in the city. This trip to see Jo was just one of so, so many, all packed into those final months of 2019. My head and my heart were reeling.

Jo and I didn't know when we would ever see each other again after this trip. Try as we might, we could only find one night free to carve out together, so we decided to splash out on a really posh hotel. Coming from quite simple living conditions, we were giddy with excitement. But when we looked at the prices of meals in the hotel restaurant, our jaws dropped. Hence the third note on the calendar—*bring lunch*.

We'd agreed to mitigate the expense by packing one lunch each: one for the Friday when we arrived and one for the Saturday before we left. That would just leave the Friday dinner for us to dine as fine ladies in the hotel restaurant. And so the night before the trip, I put on my chef's hat and collected a sample of my favorite ingredients: fresh basil leaves, feta cheese, olives, and sundried tomatoes imported from Italy. I made a stunning pasta salad which I thought was worthy of such an occasion as this.

The very last note on the calendar read *bring G&T*. Living in a Muslim-majority country, both of us had chosen to forego alcohol while on location. However, in our pre-cross-cultural lives we had both liked to have a glass of wine or a gin and tonic. Sometimes we would meet up in each other's rooms at our annual conference and have a quiet drink and catch up. We weren't breaking any rules, but still, we would giggle like naughty school girls before taking a sip. Good wine was impossible to find (or afford) in those parts, but the sense of connection to our past lives and the relief of acting "normally" without a view to watching neighbors always lifted our spirits.

Jo and I shared so much, so freely, with each other: our love for Indonesia, our love for Jesus, our hopes, our disappointments, our free time and holiday time, our enjoyment of food and drink, our culture shock, and our British and Australian senses of humor. Our times together, as well as our voice messages, were characterized by raw vulnerability, grace, deep mutual encouragement as sisters in Christ, enthusiastic story-telling, and snorts of laughter.

But I was looking forward to this particular get-together with Jo for still another reason. On top of my grief over leaving Indonesia, I was struggling with the deep and private grief of losing a baby. Two months earlier, our fourth child was born after just ten weeks gestation. It had happened the very same week we learned we were leaving Indonesia. It was a heart-breaking time for our family as both these griefs merged into one. During these heavy months, strong emotions constantly surged beneath my surface. I desperately longed to talk out my grief with Jo—face-to-face at last.

Finally, the day arrived. As we stepped together into the hotel foyer with its marble pillars and impeccably dressed reception staff, we marveled and grinned at each other. A porter carried our bags to our room, and we followed along, bouncy as spring lambs, taking in the spiral staircases and fresh cleanliness of the hotel—jarringly beautiful after the dust and chaos of the city streets.

When we got to our tidy twin bedroom, we put down our bags and began to unpack. I passed Jo the piano stool, mentally checking it off my to-do list. Once our clothes and books had found their places, we pulled out the lunches.

"Which shall we have first?" Jo asked.

"Well, let's have a look and see," I said. "I've brought a pasta salad." I pulled out the salad, took off the lid, and held it out for her inspection.

Jo leaned forward to look and sighed. "That looks *delicious*," she said. I beamed.

"What did you bring?" I said.

"Well . . ." she said, and pulled out a small container. She took off the lid, and I leaned forward to peer inside.

It was dry couscous.

"Couscous?" I said. "Good idea. We can cook it with water from the kettle. What else did you bring?"

"Well," she said, "I also brought some raisins."

I looked at her for a few seconds, waiting for the next component of the dish. After a while, I realized that nothing more was forthcoming.

"Is that it?" I said and started to laugh.

"Well, yes." She looked baffled for a minute. "It's not much, is it?" she grinned.

I was too surprised to know what to say. I mean, we'd talked about food lots, and I'd never known her to eat bizarrely plain things before.

After a second, Jo said, "So which one should we have today?"

Was it the work of the Holy Spirit? Or was it all just too much for one woman to hold in? At that moment, the utter joy of being in Jakarta with my friend, the incomprehensibly bland lunch she had prepared, and her innocent question of which one we would want to eat, erupted out of my chest in loud and unstoppable laughter.

I choked out, "We'll have mine, of course!" and for several minutes after, I was laughing so hard I couldn't speak. Tears ran down my face, and my cheeks were burning. Jo was laughing too—but I was completely out of control.

I had heard the phrase, "I laughed so hard that I cried," but that day was the first time I had experienced it. There in that hotel room, completely gripped by laughter, at some point I started to sob—heaving, body-wracking sobs, tears still streaming down. Snot started streaming too, and I fumbled around for tissues.

"Are you crying now?" Jo asked, looking up in surprise.

"I think I am!" I said. I tried to catch my breath. "I'll be okay in a second!"

But it took a lot longer than a second. For a full five minutes I was laughing and crying and sobbing and blowing, releasing months of built-up grief and loss and hope and excitement, letting go of all of the passion and all of the need to keep a lid on it and all of the administrative tasks and all of the needs of my children and husband and all the wondering what God could possibly be doing and all of the excitement of a night away with Jo and all the emotion of the hot heaving streets outside and the perfectly folded white sheets inside and the pasta salad and the giving of a really nice piano stool and the curving marble staircases and a dry bed of couscous sprinkled with raisins. All of it burst from within me like a solar flare, and I was utterly at the mercy of the laugh.

I came down to earth like a piece of ash floating down from a bonfire, weak and shaky, utterly depleted but calm. Jo and I headed out to find a spot by the pool to make a start on the pasta salad. We went on to have a delightful weekend of food, drink, and non-stop storytelling, accompanied, sometimes, by trickling tears or starbursts of laughter.

I never saw that container of couscous reemerge or the raisins either; perhaps Jo was afraid that if she brought them out, I'd fall to pieces again. I can't remember what we did for lunch the next day. But every time I remember that moment in the hotel room, I find myself smiling, then grinning, then chuckling.

And sometimes, I find myself crying, too—crying for the sheer joy of having such a life and such a friend as Jo.

Chapter 31

FINDING FRIENDSHIP ABROAD

By Rachael Kabagaba

I moved abroad at twenty-eight years old to teach at a school in Kenya I had never visited before, to students I didn't know, in a country I was entirely unfamiliar with. This, coupled with the fact that I had withdrawn from a young singles ministry in Houston that regularly gathered hundreds of young adults under one roof, left me feeling isolated. As I boarded the plane from Atlanta, Georgia, to Nairobi, Kenya, questions rushed through my mind: *Would I be okay in Kenya? Would my ministry work be successful? Would I be safe?* And perhaps scariest of all, *Will I have friends?*

Friendships have never been easy for me. For as long as I can remember, I've longed for but rarely had a good friend who sticks by my side through thick and thin. My friends in elementary, middle, and high school chatted with me during the day but didn't call me at night. To be fair, I didn't call them either. In college, I joined a sorority with the promise that the girls would be my "sisters for life." Our friendships were fickle at best then and non-existent now.

After college, I moved from Michigan to Houston, Texas, for a job. I spent seven years working hard to build friendships. I did everything by the book, going to events, interacting with new and old friends, showing up in hard times. It was finally there, in Houston, where I found my life-long Christian companions.

In the process of considering missions, friendships were a recurrent thought on my mind. As a single woman, I relied heavily upon my community to meet my relational needs. Moving to a school of mostly families didn't sound like a good way to get those needs met.

Nonetheless, through the doubt, God nudged me towards Kenya. In the months leading up to the move, I pleaded to God for friends. Over and over again, my prayer was for God to provide at least one person that I could do life with. One friend who would shed tears and share laughter with me. If I could have that, I knew I'd be okay.

Shortly after arriving in Kenya in August 2022, I quickly bonded with a few other singles my age who were also new to our ministry location. We created regular meal, coffee, and hangout sessions. I was thrilled to have found friends so fast. We formed a close-knit group, doing everything together and nothing without the others.

Everything seemed fine until we took our first vacation together with several others to the Kenyan coast in early October. Surrounded by tropical trees and crystal blue water, I saw for the first time that the others in my "clique" had a bond with each other that I didn't have with any of them. Though we all spent time together, it appeared to me as if I was on the fringes of the group. On top of that, I knew they were hanging out in smaller groups without me. They clicked with each other in a way that I didn't. As the vacation went on, this realization grew more and more apparent. By the time we boarded the little plane from Diani to Nairobi, it was obvious that my new friendships weren't as deep as I had thought. I cried for days when I got home.

I learned an important lesson through this group: Your first friends don't have to be your final friends. What comes first may not last, and that's okay. On the surface, it seemed like we had everything in common that would bond us: similar age, stage of life, and the newness to the field. Nonetheless, while they were a good fit for each other, I wasn't a good fit in the group.

My head knew this fact, but my heart struggled to accept it. I grieved for weeks over the awareness that I didn't have a solid group here after all. I continued to hang out with the group for the rest of the year, all the while living in the reality that they were not my "people." At first, I despised them for their relationship. I wanted with them what they had with each other. After time and prayer, I learned another important lesson: Not everyone on your team is going to be your close friend, and that's okay.

In mid-October, our staff received a plea for help. A conference would be happening in December, about one week before Christmas, in Uganda, and the organizers wondered if anyone at our location would be willing to help out. I sat in the local coffee shop, reading and re-reading the email. Uganda is my home country—my parents were born, raised, educated, and married there. It wouldn't be a burden to go. In addition, my dad was already planning to come out from the U.S. I could spend time with him and my extended family.

I mentally shuffled through the few individuals I knew who might even consider coming. The few girls in my not-so-tight-knit clique were out. A single friend Katherine already had plans. Maybe my friend Amanda would be open to tagging along? I hadn't asked Amanda to do anything like this. We weren't close. We hung out on occasion, studying Scripture with a mutual friend once a week and talking after school. On occasion, we would chat at her house which was just on the other side of mine. As duplex neighbors, we couldn't have been closer. Having been in missions at our location one year longer than me, she wasn't included in the new member group.

I decided I had nothing to lose. I apprehensively approached her soon after reading the email. To my surprise, she said she had been considering the trip as well. At that point, it was as good as done. We were going to Uganda together for the conference, and Amanda would spend a few weeks with my family for the Christmas holiday.

By the time the conference rolled around, Amanda and I had grown tremendously in our friendship. We were doing more activities together and found that even though we are polar opposites in nearly every way, we get along well and enjoy each other's company. Even though we had shared many great moments over the past few months, I was nervous about traveling with her. It had been years since I had gone on an international trip with a friend, and I had never gone on one with someone I had known for only a few months. We were taking a gamble; if this trip worked out, it would cement our friendship. If it didn't, our friendship would flounder just as fast as it had flourished, and we would have to see each other every single day afterwards since our homes were connected. The saying "high risk, high reward" couldn't have been more true.

Our trip started with a one-night stay at my uncle's house in Kampala. We ate the feast my aunt had prepared for us at 11 P.M., exhausted from a day of travel. We collapsed into bed without much discussion. A few hours later, we rose before dawn to meet up with conference goers. Together, we'd take a private bus for twelve hours to Arua. Amanda and I chose our seats (me, window; her, aisle) and braced for the long drive. We didn't speak much except for the occasional, "Hey, look at that animal!" On the bus of around thirty strangers, it was a comfort to have Amanda by my side. When we finally reached the hotel, we settled into our separate rooms and called it a night.

For the next few days, I watched over the pre-teen group, a small but mighty bunch of mostly boys who wanted to spend their days watching Netflix, while Amanda corralled the toddlers. We debriefed during meals and spent our few hours off-duty by the pool or in the hotel lobby getting to know the other attendees. The conference was wonderful, but for me, the best was still to come: time spent with my family in the western Ugandan countryside.

Having visited Uganda my whole life, I knew exactly what to expect. Amanda, on the other hand, had never been to Uganda or any rural African village. I couldn't wait to see her reaction.

Right after the conference, we connected with my dad and went straight to his family in the village. As soon as we pulled into the compound, my school-aged cousins swarmed Amanda, touching her skin and calling her *mzungu*! My grandma, aunts, and uncles also gave her a warm, friendly greeting. This was the first time I had brought a friend to my family. They, and I, were excited to have a visitor.

The next week and a half was a whirlwind of driving various distances, visiting relatives and business developments all over the area. Through it all, Amanda had a cheerful, positive attitude. I loved watching her bond with my older cousins and play games with my younger cousins. She truly seemed to enjoy the country and my family and spending Christmas with them. The highlight for both of us was watching the entire process of a goat slaughtering, then driving to several family members' homes and delivering different parts of the animal as a Christmas gift. It was at that moment when I knew we'd both remember this trip forever.

Our trip to Uganda secured my friendship with Amanda in a way that no amount of coffee dates ever could have. Through traveling and volunteering, we were able to see different sides of one another. We had the laugh-till-you-pee-your-pants moments and the somber, reflective moments. Mostly, we learned that we enjoy one another. Over the course of time since that trip, Amanda and I have grown into a dynamic duo. We do nearly everything together. We've even traveled beyond Uganda, to Egypt and northern Kenya. Through her, I can see that God answered my prayer of finding my "one true friend."

One specific time that makes us laugh as we look back is the Christmas Eve goat slaughter. As is customary in our culture, my dad selected two goats to slaughter and deliver to relatives as a Christmas present. Amanda had never heard or seen anything like it. We watched in mild terror as a young man dragged the chosen goat to a tree to be hung. At one point, while skinning the goat, the young man looked at her horror, smiling and laughing. We couldn't help but laugh too. A few hours later, in the black of night, we stopped at house after house, delivering choice portions of the goat to my aunts, cousins, and grandparents. When we look back on that day, which we often do, we laugh as we recall the oddity of a new cultural experience and the fellowship that day forged between us.

Time on the field hasn't been easy. Just like anyone else, I've had my ups and downs. I feel blessed that I've had Amanda by my side for nearly all of it. She's seen me at my best and worst and still chooses to spend time with me. Navigating life on the field isn't easy, but it's easier when you have an "Amanda" walking beside you.

Chapter 32

GOD DELIGHTS IN ME

By Kristi A.

There are moments in our lives when we seem to delight in every moment—a simple cup of coffee is enough to spark joy and give us a glimpse of the goodness of our creator. Particularly as women serving cross-culturally, we know we often find delight in our host culture and the work God has called us to. There are seasons when our host culture bumps against us, but it causes laughter to spill out. Our faith feels vibrant and colorful and always right at the surface so that it overflows. The difficulties of ministry slide like water off a duck's back because of the immense delight we feel in our calling.

But we also know there are seasons when this is not the case. Those glimmers of delight seem to be hidden far beneath what we are experiencing. Bumping against our host culture no longer brings laughter but rather leaves bruises in what feels like a personal attack. Delight seems a foreign concept—we doubt God's goodness, and our faith feels as vibrant as a desert in drought.

The last few years in Cambodia were definitely that for me. Life was a lot and difficult in many ways. I married my wonderful husband in the living room of our home in our host country, away from family and friends due to COVID-19. I joined an anti-trafficking organization and opened a new daycare ministry. I had multiple tropical diseases (simultaneously), COVID-19 three times, a motorcycle accident, and developed a long-term chronic illness that still has not been diagnosed.

We moved to a new area to live among a minority Muslim group where a bat lived in our living room and we had no washing machine. We had severe financial troubles, and I had to close my ministry due to health issues. Needless to say, delight is not a word I would use to describe any part of my life. I felt dry, and God felt far away, sometimes even cruel.

At one of my lowest points, I was reading a book on prayer. The author mentioned that we often pray weak prayers, because we don't believe God will answer them—specifically, that He doesn't care about us enough to answer them. He talked about how God actually delights in us and desires to bless us with things that may seem "silly" or "unimportant" to others. He gave a challenge to pray a prayer that feels so silly that it almost seems wrong to pray and see what God will do.

In a moment of desperation I practically shouted at God, "Fine! You say you love me, that you care? If that's true, give me a cat. Prove it by changing my husband's mind. I'm done talking to him or You about it." I prayed but had low expectations of anything happening.

Without background, this seems like an absurd prayer. (Let's be honest—even with background, it sounds absurd!) But I am a huge animal lover, and before I moved overseas, there was never a moment in my life when I did not have a pet. I really missed having a pet in my home. I often begged my husband to get a cat, but he firmly refused— we traveled too much, there are too many ways for animals to die here, we can't afford it, etc. He actually asked me to stop bringing it up because it was becoming a point of contention. For my husband to agree to a cat was no small feat.

The day after I prayed, our house became the eleventh plague. Massive rats began to invade our house. Multiple times a day I would hear a shout from my husband that another huge rat was near him. They only seemed interested in exploring when my husband was around—I never saw one once. It was driving him crazy.

The last straw came about a week later when a rat narrowly missed my husband's foot as he cooked dinner. I heard a weak, "That's it—we're getting a cat," from the kitchen.

I didn't want to give him any time to change his mind, so I immediately messaged a local shelter about cats up for adoption. I was there the next day looking at the options.

On the way I prayed that God would point out the most playful, cuddly cat there. When I walked up to the table where the cats were playing, one placed its head on my stomach and began purring loudly. I knew it was the one.

During the tuk tuk ride home, I couldn't stop crying. Every

time I looked at her I could hear God whispering, I love you; I love you; I love you. You are My delight.

We ended up naming her after the unofficially recognized Saint Gertrude, whose miracle was praying the rats out of an infested town. She lived up to her namesake. We only saw one rat after we got her—it ran into our house, saw Gertie, squeaked dramatically, and turned to leave the way it came.

Gertie has brought so much joy into our lives. She is mischievous and cuddly and loves to play soccer (or football!) with rolled up napkins. She plays fetch and loves to sit in our neighbor's potted plants. We call her the "M" cat because she has helped facilitate relationships with our neighbors due to her silly antics. She is a comfort and delight not only to me but also to every person who enters our home. She always lies with me on the days when the chronic pain is too much to get out of bed.

She is a living, breathing reminder that God truly does love me—enough to prove it to a doubting daughter by sending rats to her husband.

I laugh when Gertie steals my husband's pen as he works, and I know God chuckles alongside me. I can feel His favor and delight shining on me as I sip tea and cuddle Gertie. In quiet moments of prayer we still laugh together over the rats only my husband saw. In moments when my faith feels weak, Gertie sits on my lap, and I hear that steady whisper again, *I love you; I love you; I love you.*

Finally understanding God's love for me has completely changed my life. I pray bolder prayers because I know He is faithful to respond. I trust Him when things get difficult because I know that just as He delights with me, He grieves with me as well. I am less hesitant to obey because my Father gives good gifts.

The delight that has flooded my soul because of a simple cat is a testimony to God's goodness. I am still flabbergasted that the God who created the universe also created us weak humans with desires that He longs to fill. He doesn't just want what we do for Him; He wants us. How can I not rejoice and overflow with delight when that God chose me?

Will you dare to ask God to show His delight to you? Will you be brave enough to pray the prayer that feels too big because of how small it seems? I pray God showers you with delight in ways that are specific to you—whether it's a certain ingredient showing up in your local supermarket, your favorite brand of tea that you can never find, or your favorite flowers blooming where they normally don't—whatever your version of "Gertie" is.

> "The Lord directs the steps of the godly. He delights in every detail of their lives." Psalm 37:23 NLT

Chapter 33

LAUGHTER IS ANESTHESIA

By Lillian Joyce

I sat in my normal seat for our team meeting. In front of me was the coffee table laden with a thermos filled with coffee, a substance I didn't like to drink. Across the table from me in IKEA chairs sat George and Andrea, the couple who led the team. Other chairs and sofas were filled by the rest of our team.

Every week we sat in the same circle in the same order. We discussed and planned activities for the NGO with which we worked.

I thought today would be the same. Nothing looked any different than before. The coffee and my teammates were all arranged in the same order. Small chatter bounced happily from wall to wall as we waited for the leader to start the meeting.

"We have an announcement to share," George began.

All eyes turned towards him. Not at all ready for the words he was about to say.

"Andrea and I have accepted a new job offer. This will be our last team meeting with you."

Stunned, we sat in silence. Normally there are some indications or some simple clues that a person will decide to leave. I had seen nothing.

"Why?" a member of the team broke the silence.

"We have been thinking a long time about it. We decided it was the right decision."

He paused. We all waited for his answer to continue.

"I didn't plan anything for today," George said, "I figured since this news would be a surprise to you, I'd give you this team meeting time to ask questions."

Silence penetrated my ears. The air felt heavy around me. I had no questions. Shock and logical questions never mixed well together in my experience. Games. That was the answer to this terrible situation. Laughter. We needed to experience the joyful unity we had once felt.

"We should play a game," I heard my voice speak to the group.

Members of the team looked at me in pity, like I was trying to break the sacred moment of sadness.

This wasn't a sacred moment. It was sheer shock.

I remembered from my years growing up as Third Culture Kid the special goodbye moments of playing one more round of the card game Scum with my friends before we had to say a final goodbye, creating funny faces on my violin case while my friend waited with me in the airport for the check-in to open, and making impossible statements about secretly becoming a stowaway in an uncle's large suitcase.

Each picture brought a smile to my lips. Creating joyful last memories had been just as important as allowing myself to feel the heaviness of saying goodbye.

A few teammates tried to break the silence by asking questions. "When will you be leaving?" "Where will you be moving?" "What is your new job?" Yet once the answers were given, silence once more filled the room.

"We should play a game," I said again.

"What would we play?" another member asked, trying to humor my request.

"Dutch Blitz would be a good game."

I received a quiet smile in reply.

Inside my head, I left the uncomfortable silence to recall the fun game nights George had organized twice for our team. That first session, we had played Battleship Extreme. The goal was to keep out of range from enemy fire while trying to fire at the enemy.

We played women against men.

Voices had whispered, "I think they are here." "Let's fire." "Wait, make sure our engines are capable of firing."

Confusion. Stressed giggles. And finally a sigh, "We sank." The men had won.

"Next time you won't win!" we promised, laughing. "We will understand the game much better. This was just our first time."

We didn't play again. I don't know why. Instead, the next time we played a new game: Burrito. The essence of this game was not to get hit by a squishy toy burrito. Women screamed, and men tried to look brave while burritos flew about the room. I laughed and laughed until I was gasping for breath.

"Well, let's end early for today." George's voice brought me back to the living room full of shocked teammates. Standing up, I said goodbye, knowing that this last team meeting with George and Andrea would be stored into my memory as a depressing gray wall.

At the next meeting, though two chairs now stood empty, they remained the center of our conversation. The injured questions that had been covered by shock now surfaced: "Why didn't they give us more warning?" and "How do we move forward?"

The following weeks, we each became little islands as we tried to understand and process in our own way what had just happened. A new team leader, Tim, stepped up to the plate. Yet instead of the once trusting group of people we had been, the lingering questions penetrated our relationships: "Who will be the next one to leave? How can I protect myself from the gray wall of goodbyes?"

One morning as we planned some kids' games for the NGO, Tim said, "Remember, next Wednesday is our monthly dinner."

The next week, we straggled in, bringing food to share. We chatted about non-important things like the weather, how our old team leader was fairing, and the troubling current events.

Finally, once the food was all eaten and the small talk had died down, the leader said, "Let's clear the table; I brought a game to play."

He pulled out three packs of playing cards. Throwing them upside-down in a most disgraceful manner on the table, he began to mix them up like a pot of soup. "All right, everyone needs four cards, upside-down," he instructed as he began to explain the rules of the game.

It was a simple game. Not like the battleship or the burrito games. The goal was to simply get rid of your cards. But there was a catch. We didn't know what was underneath the four cards that were upside down. It was a running chance. Would they cause you to pick up the whole pile or help you win the game?

Slowly as we began to end the first round, laughter began to ring in our team once again. "I bet it is a king!" "Should I flip it, or should I wait?"

Exclamations of surprise or dismay rose in response to each mystery card turned. The hours turned. We did not notice them. The gray wall that had formed within our team began to crumble.

"Let's play this game when we eat dinner together next month," a teammate exclaimed as we parted ways.

"Yes," other voices, including mine, chimed in.

Next month and the next we played the same game. We created new tricks and strategies, trying to beat the mysterious cards. "You tell me which card to flip first; you were right last time." New exclamations rose when by chance our strategies worked.

In between the monthly games, once a week we continued to meet in the same living room facing the same silent IKEA chairs. We still talked of the day that George and Andrea left so suddenly. We still tried to understand. We still gave sadness the parking place close to the door. Yet our dose of monthly laughter became anesthesia for the pain. It gave us time to heal without remaining stuck in the never-ending questions.

We became a team again, one that could look forward to the time when we would all gather to simply enjoy laughing together, to the time when Tim's hand would wiggle the mystery card back and forth saying in his comical way, "Should I flip it or should I not," and then to watch each one of us one by one crumble into astonished laughter when he would win the game by sheer chance.

*Names and places changed

Chapter 34

A HARD LAUGH

By Karen Lubbers-Odel

"He will once again fill your mouth with laughter and your lips with shouts of joy". —Job 8:21 NLT

Let's be honest, my laughter can quickly pause a room full of people. I come from a long lineage of rambunctious laughers, and when we get together, it's a wonderful surround sound system of joy. I'm often told, "Oh, I knew you were here; I heard you laughing!" Those comments come even when I don't remember opening my mouth to laugh.

In Bible college, I remember how an older student would always stand up in the cafeteria and jokingly call out my name because I had once again disrupted his eating pattern with my normal daily laugh. Just the other day, after a quick burst of laughter over who knows what, my friend said, "I needed that today, thanks for laughing." Those spurts of laughter are often short-lived, but, of course, there are also those times when I laugh so loud and long that my cheeks hurt and my stomach muscles have a good workout.

Often I have found that laughter invites people in or brings smiles to heavy faces on weary days. Laughter lightens moods and softens hearts. It's medicine for the soul and joy to the ears. That's why I was profoundly shocked when I was the only one in the crowd not laughing and wondering what I had missed.

In 2009, I had been in Uganda only a few short weeks when I was invited to ride along in an NGO vehicle to visit former child soldiers deep in the village. We traveled from Soroti to Obalanga, sixty-four kilometers in ninety minutes, to encourage youth who had recently escaped from being war victims.

Joseph Kony and the LRA, Lord's Resistance Army, had swept through the northern tribes of Uganda and captured young people along the way to be soldiers, wives, and servants. The LRA is a militant group that has been active since the 1980s, trying to wage a war of attrition on the people and government of Uganda and surrounding countries. From 2003–2007, Joseph Kony (an Acholi by birth) led his rebel group into the Teso region, amongst the Ateso tribe.

Those four or more years were a very hard season in northern Uganda, and my colleagues at the NGO and I were coming to Obalanga to share hope, both practically and spiritually. We had brought along groundnut (peanut) seeds and cassava cuttings. We also came with Bibles and messages of the forgiveness and hope we find in Christ Jesus. Counselors had come to share with the community about how to deal with trauma, especially when there was still so much fresh hurt and distrust.

Under a wide-spanning mango tree, a large community of people gathered, sitting in wooden school desks or on mats. The LRA had been pushed out of the area a year or two earlier, but you could still see deep suffering and pain on the locals' faces. These former child soldiers appreciated that we had come, and as a sign of thanksgiving, they wanted to put on a simple drama to show us what life was like in captivity.

Under the bright African sun, the reenactment started with people sitting around campfires, sharing stories with a smile on their faces. Women were cooking food over a fire surrounded by three stones and a large clay pot. Children were giggling and running around. Slowly we started to see the enemy encroaching from the tall grasses beyond. Fears, screams, and tears began as people jumped and ran in different directions. What started out as a lighthearted play soon had me on the edge of the bench; my sheltered past in rural Canada could never even imagine a life like this.

Some of the young guys who were acting had given their lives to Jesus, and so there was a little more twinkle in their eyes as they squatted through grasses, aiming their guns at people. But a few faces weren't in acting mode anymore. I saw scary anger in their eyes as the story unfolded. No messing with these young men. Charms were put around their necks, and foreheads were anointed with oil. The LRA is not just any kind of army; there's a lot of wizardry and witchcraft involved.

Soon the boys were producing machine guns made from wood and rubber bands that, when they were shot, would snap so loud we all had the hair on our arms go up. Baby powder dispersed from the guns to make the shots look even more real. The youth grabbed each other roughly and continued showing us the struggles and hardships of war. After wreaking havoc in their villages and some killing their own family members, as was the leader's command, the youth were tied and dragged for many kilometers.

Was this really a drama? The faces were too serious to be acting. I started to realize how intensely real this had been for these formerly innocent youth. While my eyes were being clouded with tears, I started to hear laughter all around me. I looked around and saw the crowd chuckling, some hiding their smiles behind closed fists. What?! Another scream brought me back to the "play" happening in an open field. More scenes of war, abuse, rape, and hardship were appearing before me as drops of water poured from my eyes and down my cheeks. *Lord, these young people have seen and endured so much! Lord, thank You for rescuing them and bringing them home* were the prayers in my heart.

Some of the youth escaped in the night, whether impromptu or well-planned. Others were able to sneak away when the whole army was forced to cross deep rivers. The drama was over as the rest of the army marched further back into the bushes. I sat in stunned silence while the crowd's laughter got louder. I bent over to my neighbor and emotionally asked, "Why is everyone laughing? That was not funny at all! This is scary and serious stuff!"

The response came back. "What else can we do but laugh? We don't want to cry anymore! We are glad our youth are home. We praise God the war is over here! And we still hope for the return of more of those who were captured." Laughter was one practical way for them to find courage and to hold on to hope. Psalm 42:5 says, "Why am I discouraged? Why is my heart so sad? I will put my hope in God! I will praise him again" (NLT).

Now that I have been in Uganda for more than fourteen years, I am starting to get used to the local people chuckling when I might tend to be serious. Uganda's laughter can be seen as group therapy or a community's response to overcoming hardship. It's also understood as a way of relating to the dead, a coping mechanism that helps everyone conquer the pain that was experienced. I think the Ugandan people have it right. We should laugh more often because the "joy of the Lord is [our] strength" (Nehemiah 8:10 NLT). I no longer respond so emotionally but chuckle under my breath, wondering if I will ever culturally learn to laugh as they do.

> *"We were filled with laughter, and we sang for joy. And the other nations said, 'What amazing things the Lord has done for them.'" Psalm 126:2 NLT*

Chapter 35

JOY IN UNEXPECTED MOMENTS

By Rebecca Nolley

I'm not a natural runner.

I guess you could say I became a runner out of desperation. It has become my way of escape—a stress relief, a way to get out of the house, and a way to have some alone time. This necessity grew in the midst of moving to Uganda, starting a ministry, adopting two children, and homeschooling five children. The need was real.

When I started running, I found that I actually enjoyed it not only because it gave me some reprieve from the chaos of my life but also because I found a running partner. My Kenyan friend was much faster and had much more endurance than I did, but she put up with me and pushed me to improve. In fact, she pushed me to the extent of signing up for a half marathon in the capital city of Kampala, while she ran a full marathon.

During training we did our long runs on Saturday mornings when we had more time. On one particular Saturday morning, I was running nine miles while she was aiming for eighteen. I decided that I would run the nine and then just get a *boda* (basically a motorcycle taxi) to take me back while she ran back to get the extra miles.

The plan seemed good at the time until I realized how far out we had actually gone into the bush of northern Uganda. When she turned to run back, there were no bodas in sight; in fact, there was no one in sight. I started walking, too exhausted to run, hoping that a boda would soon pass by. Minute after minute ticked by, and no boda. At this point I was feeling desperate, hot, sticky with sweat, and completely worn out.

Finally, a boda came into view. Unfortunately, I didn't notice the goat strapped to the back until after I flagged it down. I asked the man if he was going into town. He said he had to drop off this goat at a wedding on his way to town but could take me. Like I said, I was desperate. So I hopped onto the boda with the goat in my lap.

As we started off, the goat looked up at me and gave a pathetic bleat, seeming to know that he was on his way to be lunch. His fur stuck to my sweaty skin as he continued to call out what sounded like "maaa" as we careened down the road. As the wind whipped up the red dust of the road to add another nice layer to the goat hair that was now plastered to my skin, I looked around expecting to see a movie camera recording this bizarre situation. No movie cameras. Just the tall grass of the African plains and me and my goat. I started laughing with the realization of how ridiculous I looked. The boda driver, who probably already thought I was a bit crazy to be running so far out in the bush, must have thought I was completely insane as he drove this laughing white woman with a goat in her lap to a wedding.

As we arrived at the wedding, I ducked my head and hid, knowing what a mess I looked like.

I was dirty, smelly, and definitely did not belong at a wedding. I imagined those wedding guests wondering what on earth I was doing there but also doing what was culturally appropriate and inviting me to join. Thankfully I was able to avoid attending the wedding, and once the goat was delivered to the appropriate people, the driver took me the rest of the way to my home.

I wished with all my heart that a secret camera could have captured that moment, but it will always remain in my memory as a moment that brought me joy. We can find joy in those unexpected moments—in the mundane or seemingly normal actions of the day and in the awkward situations we find ourselves in. Even though there were no witnesses to this moment (besides the goat and boda driver), I knew God could see. Was He laughing too? I think so.

As women on the field, we can get bogged down with the heaviness of life—the pain others are in, the magnitude of the needs, and the hardships of living in a different culture away from our family and friends. It's small moments like these that remind us of the fullness of joy that we have. His presence is ever with us, and He is guiding us each step of the way. As Psalm 16:11 declares, "You make known to me the path of life; in your presence there is fullness of joy; at your right hand are pleasures forevermore" (ESV).

God's presence is always with us bringing us true joy, no matter what path He has us on and no matter what circumstances we are in. We might feel like we are in the middle of nowhere, stranded and alone, but He is right there. And He'll provide for us, even if it's a boda ride with a goat.

REAL SUPERMARKET MOMENTS:
AT THE CHECKOUT...

Chapter 36

DID YOU KNOW WE HAVE A DRYER?

By Sara Pascal

We were only one week into the very necessary, heartbreaking work of aiding Ukrainian refugees when I swore at one of our house guests. Many believers in Moldova, foreign and local, were scrambling to support those flooding out of Ukraine after they were invaded by Russia. By the end of five weeks, our little 700-square-foot apartment would see more than thirty house guests. During that time, we also drove dozens of people from the border to the capital; purchased shoes, clothes, bedding, train, and bus tickets; facilitated housing; and so much more. Needless to say, even after just a week, we were stressed and emotionally and mentally taxed.

We had been praying for a new vehicle, and our sending church provided funds for a seven-passenger minivan. It came at the perfect time! My husband Sasha drove down to the border crossing where Moldova is nearest to Odessa and tried to convince people we were a safe choice to help them. During these first few weeks of the war there were no organizations, governments, or nonprofits helping those who crossed the border. The border was chaotic, flooded not only with amazing people giving their time and gas but also with swindlers charging refugees hundreds of euros for a two-hour car ride to Moldova's capital.

Sasha offered to drive people back to the city to catch a bus or help find a place to crash for the night. His greatest tool in convincing people to trust him was a homemade "Welcome to Moldova" sign our kids, ages nine and eleven, had colored in English, Russian, and Ukrainian. Many commented later that they trusted Sasha because he had kids.

One of the first families that arrived at our house was a young couple and their small daughter. The husband went out in the city during the day to try to find a solution for their situation, but the wife, Svetlana, stayed at our apartment with her daughter. Mornings and evenings we sat with the family around the table discussing options for their family's future. My Russian, however, is limited. Since arriving in Moldova years ago, I had concentrated on learning the state language of Romanian and had been using the Russian I knew less and less. But as the need arose, all of my Russian words began stirring in my mind.

Everything else was stirring too. No one was sleeping. We were transporting people at all hours of the night, buying mattresses and food for local churches, hosting, making phone calls to find beds for those we couldn't host—and on top of that, we worried about the possibility of an invasion here. Both our family and the refugees we were hosting were just trying to keep it together.

And that's when it happened.

Svetlana was carrying a tub of washed laundry onto the balcony to hang them to dry, her brow furrowed in anxiety. I came bustling around the corner and ran right into her.

"Hey Svetlana, you know we have a . . ." and I wanted to continue that sentence in Russian with the word dryer. But that isn't what came to me, and it isn't what popped out of my mouth.

Since to my untrained ear the beginning sounds were similar, I ended up saying "Hey, Svetlana, you know we have a b****?" And I stopped and looked at her. My face got red; I knew exactly what I'd said but couldn't find the right word. I ran quickly to the balcony and pointed at our dryer. And then we both burst out laughing.

The insurmountable stress of war and pressing decisions was put aside, for just a minute, and laughter came. Svetlana repeated the word for dryer to me several times while I copied her and laughed.

For those six weeks most of the world with its huge nonprofits and refugee experts were unprepared for the Ukrainian crisis, but the few believers and churches in Moldova were there saving people. I think about that time a lot. I pray often, usually with tears, for the people we met. But those sad thoughts are accompanied by laughter at this hilarious language mishap and the graciousness of Svetlana in that chaotic moment. (*Svetlana is a pseudonym. She and her family arrived in Spain and made a life for themselves since the start of the war.*)

Chapter 37

DON'T FORGET TO LAUGH

By Rachel Swan

Our life overseas has not been at all what I pictured when we first said "yes." The beauty and the richness are there, of course, but I've often had to dig deep to find them. Living in another culture and language is far from simple, has its fair share of frustrations, and includes a heaping dose of the ridiculous.

When we first moved to our current location, I had a four-year-old and an eighteen-month-old and was pregnant with our third. That first year was wrought with illness, and I became very well acquainted with the local hospital. I was exhausted from mothering littles, being pregnant, and learning how to navigate our new language and culture. Even normally simple tasks, like cooking a basic meal for my family, took much more time and energy. At the same time, we were grieving leaving our first overseas home after COVID-19 hit, not realizing when we left that we would never go back. It was a very difficult and emotional season.

Now, three years later, I would like to say that our family is thriving, but if I'm honest, that hasn't been the case for us. We have found a rhythm here, and we are learning to take it moment by moment. We have good days and particularly hard days. In all of it, I am continually learning over and over again, sometimes as if for the first time, that I am not alone. That my God has not left me here—although it sometimes feels that way. And that our ability to laugh in the middle of the struggle can be one of His greatest gifts to us. I don't always initially respond in laughter to some of the challenges we face, but most of the time I can look back and at least chuckle a little at some of the ridiculous experiences we've walked through. And I've seen and lived some pretty ridiculous things!

As any language learner can tell you, and perhaps even more so for those of us struggling to learn a language on not enough sleep while juggling small children (sometimes literally), making a fool of yourself is easy to do. Although I tend towards perfectionism, thankfully, I've learned to laugh at myself, sometimes as others are laughing at me too.

One of my first major blunders happened early on in my language journey. I bought what I thought were pull-ups at our neighborhood market, but they turned out to be diapers. If anyone has ever tried convincing a toddler to wear diapers instead of their normal "night night undies," you understand my dismay and my determination to exchange them for pull-ups. So I did what any good language learner would do—I used Google Translate to figure out how to say, "I don't want diapers, I want pull-ups. Can I exchange these, please?"

I practiced it over and over before walking into the store. I had recently been told by my language tutor that I had a surprisingly good accent for a foreigner, so I was extra confident as I set the bag of diapers on the counter. I looked at the cashier, smiled, and said in my best accent, "I don't want diapers, I want pull-ups. Can I exchange these, please?" She stared at me, wide-eyed without responding. She's probably shocked to see a foreigner speaking her language, I thought to myself. So I repeated myself. This time a little louder and a little more slowly, just to be sure I got the accent right. Again, she stared at me without saying anything, but a giggle slipped out. This wasn't completely out of the ordinary; some people thought it was cute when I tried speaking to them in their language, so I thought maybe she was just overwhelmed with my cute self.

At this point there was a line forming at the cash register, and I started feeling a little less confident—maybe my accent was off. I decided to give it one more go, so I spoke slowly and clearly and said, "I don't want diapers, I want PULL-UPS. Can I exchange these, please?" I had barely finished my sentence when the whole line, including the cashier, erupted in laughter. Now I stood wide-eyed, not sure what I had done wrong.

The girl was kind enough to help me with the exchange, and I quickly walked out of the store and immediately hopped on my phone and pulled up Google Translate. I typed in exactly what I said, and to my horror the screen seemed to scream back at me, "I don't want diapers, I want PANTIES. Can I exchange these, please?" PANTIES?! I had just asked them to exchange my pack of diapers for women's underwear.

In that moment, I pretty much had two options. I could beat myself up for my mistake and get angry that the words for panties and pull-ups are so dang similar, or I could chock it up to a pretty embarrassing language blunder and laugh at myself and think of all those people in line who now had a great story to go home and tell their families over dinner. While I chose to do the latter, I will admit that I avoided that particular store for several weeks after that!

I am now three years into my language journey, and while I now know the difference between pull-ups and panties, I still make regular language blunders. Sometimes small ones, like telling one of the neighborhood kids that her dad was "peeing" instead of "working." (Note to self: The noun for "work" cannot be used as a verb.) And sometimes larger ones, like shrugging my shoulders noncommittally when I thought my seventy-six-year-old neighbor told me that my husband was very old. He was only thirty-seven at the time, so I thought her comment quite rude considering the fact that I'm a few years older. Turns out she said he was very handsome to which I basically responded "Meh, I guess . . ." For the record (and in case he's reading this) I do think my husband is very handsome. My neighbor and I are now good friends and often laugh about this story.

As I reflect on these memories and laugh a little to myself, I also find myself tearing up. Our life here has been hard. We have faced many challenges—health struggles, discouragement, unhealthy team dynamics—and yet we have had many opportunities to laugh, to not take ourselves too seriously, nor to take our circumstances too seriously. We have been gifted with the ability to laugh at ourselves and with each other in community.

Over the last few years, I have cried a lot of tears and have imagined those tears being collected in bottles. I would have a room full by now. But I have also laughed a lot, the kind of laughter that cannot be bottled up, that overflows and pours out and brings life to places that can feel dark and lifeless. Laughter has been a sweet gift from God in this season. Laughter has helped me to remember that I am seen in all of these moments—the good, the hard and the ridiculous—by a gracious and kind Father. And I like to think that He's laughing with me too.

And so, on the days when I'm weary from the normal and mundane, when I'm exasperated by cultural differences that I find annoying, when there is tension in relationships, when there is grief and suffering, remind me to laugh. And I will try to remind you.

PRESCHOOLERS ON AIRPLANES

Chapter 38

GRACE FOR THE UNINVITED

By Amber Taube

According to one estimate, one out of every fourteen weddings will have a wedding crasher. I never wanted to be a statistic, but here I am. I crashed a wedding with my three kids.

Before you judge me too harshly, you need to understand a few things. I wasn't there for the gifts. Praise God, our supply of financial support does not necessitate theft, and I have plenty of teacups. I was not there for the food. Rice and lentils rain from the sky in my host country. I can get the contents of the buffet on any street corner for the equivalent of one U.S. dollar.

I was there because my children made jungle gyms of the furniture and wrote somber odes to boredom. The 972nd time they asked when Daddy was coming home from the village, something inside me snapped like the dead tree across the street. It would only be a few more hours, but it wasn't soon enough. I was *done*.

"We could go into town. Let's get bubble tea! Should we call someone and see if we can come over?"

I held them off for hours, content to stay under a worn fleece quilt with the word GRACE woven in varsity letters. It had gotten me through cramming for probability and statistics class, recovering from a cesarean, and weathering winter in a concrete home without central heat. GRACE would cover me until his return.

While piling up rocks and stomping around the front gate, my troop heard singing coming from a local church. My younger daughter ran all ninety-four stairs up to our fifth floor apartment. "Mom, there is a *sangati* going on right now! Can we go?"

My stony resolve pooled into a shapeless blob of butter. Didn't our resident evangelist deserve to come home to souls settled in the spirit of God? Certainly he would prefer such a welcome to a feral clutter clawing at each other's faces, scratching at the door to the outside world.

I pulled a pair of jeans over woolen leggings but left the rest of my winter uniform, a thermal top and fleece, unchanged. My hair sat in a disheveled bun atop my head. (My oldest calls this my "home hair.") We laced up and set off down the dirt road between our house and the church. Worship would be the remedy for a day full of whining, arguing, and refusing to clean up spilled paints and play dough.

The kids stomped in puddles, thrilled by the epic journey beyond the retaining walls surrounding our property. I had to admit, moving my muscles anywhere but the kitchen felt good. The sun's warmth moved through my body, prickling over my skin and settling deep in my chest.

We rounded the corner and passed a throng of toothy middle-graders dressed for school. *It is an odd time for a church service.* The thought slipped in and out of my consciousness like a butterfly inviting my attention before flitting away. Finally, we reached the source of this morning's music. A tin roof painted orange made the cement complex appear to be under construction. The humble setting reminded me of a church we helped build by the river.

We slid our shoes off by the back door. As we entered the sanctuary, I read the message on the projector: "Congratulations, Anil and Jyoti." I grabbed the kids by their hoodies and whispered, "Let's go—now!" But before confusion splashed over their faces, we'd been made.

"Jayamasiah," two *bahinis* greeted us with hands clasped. Looking at each other, eyebrows raised, they communicated the obvious question: *Do you know these people?*

I returned the greeting, then said, "I'm so sorry. My kids heard singing and wanted to fellowship." *Was I lying? Was it me who needed to speak to an adult or two? Did my desperation lead me to become an uninvited wedding guest?*

"Welcome, welcome. Sit down, please." They placed chairs behind our knees. The older teen walked toward the pastor, one long braid swinging behind her back. A huddle of men in shirts and ties met by a window, clutching cups of tea. Their lively commune was interrupted as he turned to see us. I wanted to dive down the mountainside, but there was no way out of the tunnel of smiling aunties and grannies closing in.

Pastor Bhim's teeth gleamed against the backdrop of his dark skin as he pushed through the growing crowd to meet us. "We are so happy to have you," he said. He looked each child in the eye and asked their names.

After a few minutes of niceties, I rose from my seat. "Well, it was great meeting you. We will come back another time," I said as I gripped the shoulders of my tiny people, readying the band of intruders to run for the door.

"Oh, no," he said. "You have to stay for the feast!" He waved away my excuses as if stomachs were never too full and there could be no work which must be done this very day. To my absolute horror, one of the women handed me a *brass* plate of steaming rice.

I was an honored wedding guest, and I was wearing jeans and "home hair."

Panic snaked its way around my shoulders, breaking off into energy wells seizing my fists, shoulders, and jaw. Pastor Bhim shifted my focus from the firestorm. He expressed gratitude for our willingness to share Christ with his people and probed about what it's like to leave everything familiar. He shared about the hardships of ministry in a traditional Newari community.

The aunties brought seconds and thirds of dishes they labored all day to cook but hadn't taken a bite of yet. Church members followed the pastor's lead getting to know us. Despite our differences, there was sweet kinship tugging at our shoulders, pulling us all together.

Finishing the last bites of tender chicken curry, I forgot we weren't supposed to be here. I even started to think, *Maybe we are supposed to be here.* I leaned back in my seat as if I were back under GRACE. Even in an awkward situation wearing inappropriate attire, I was at peace. It may not have been the worship we came for, but it felt holy.

I didn't want to linger long enough for the welcome to cool, so I began my rounds. I thanked each auntie, granny, and *bahini* for their service and Pastor Bhim for his kindness. I gave him my husband's phone number for future connection.

"You can't leave without meeting the bride and groom!" he protested.

Gratitude stepped over to give my pride a moment on the stage. The word *no* ran on a continuous loop beneath my top knot. *No* was louder than the Gospel choruses drawing my children here this afternoon. *No* was louder than pleas for bubble tea. *No* was louder than a tide of LEGO® raked over carpet in a frantic search for the missing piece. But *no* never made it to my lips.

Anil and Jyoti held hands and smiled at the crazy American wishing them a happy life together. My last degree of dignity crumpled like my toddler's latest art installation as I answered the list of obligatory questions.

"Mom, can we swing for a little while?" the little one begged. *No* finally bridged the space between my mouth and her ears, miniature replicas of her Dad's. Her precious request had gotten us into this mess.

We carried rice bellies home and up all ninety-four stairs, each step more labored than the last. I locked the door and crawled under GRACE. I sought access to the peace I felt an hour before with turmeric and ginger on my tongue, enveloped by the love of local saints.

Keys jingled in the front door. A flurry of feet raced to jump their dad. My husband greeted the mob while pushing past to get to me. Instead of sliding into his open arms, I shook his shoulders and said, "You'll never guess what I did."

Without pausing, I filled him in. "I crashed a wedding."

My beloved's mouth dropped open. "No, you didn't."

Wait, did I?

Chapter 39

TOGETHER: PAIN AND LAUGHTER

By Darlene Zimmerman

Three months after our move to Thailand I was lying on a doctor's table enduring intense physical pain as the doctor tried to stop the bleeding of a small mass in my cervix.

We had been in to see the doctor a few days earlier, and he had taken a biopsy of the mass. "If the bleeding doesn't stop, come back in," he told me. A couple days later the bleeding from the biopsy was not slowing down, so we headed back in. I was tired, weak, and scared as my husband, Delvin, drove me the twenty minutes to the hospital.

Once there the nurses informed us my doctor was not in. Instead, we were sent to a young gentleman with limited English who seemed as nervous as I was. We explained the best we could what was going on. He instructed me to climb on the table so he could do an examination. It was not long until I realized this was not going to be fun.

During the examination the bleeding intensified, and the

doctor became a bit frantic. In his haste to stop the bleeding, the doctor chose not to use any anesthesia as he worked to remove enough of the mass for the bleeding to stop. More nurses joined him. They bustled around handing over instruments and swabs, fanning me and waving a strong oil under my nose to help keep me from passing out. My husband left the crowded room to walk the hall and get some fresh air.

It almost made me feel panicked to not be able to understand the conversations between the doctor and the nurses. I was at their mercy.

As the doctor worked, in a quiet voice I repeatedly prayed over and over, "Jesus, help me. Jesus, help me." After about fifteen minutes of listening to this mumbling, the soft-spoken doctor said, with maybe a bit of exasperation, "I am trying to help you."

Amid the pain, a splash of cool refreshing amusement washed over me. "I am trying to help you." For some reason, this line just epitomized the craziness of the moment: the language barrier, the misunderstood prayers, the stressed nurse waving the scented swab under my nose, and a husband out walking halls to get some air. What an experience.

This moment brought smiles and shared laughter with friends in the next days and weeks as they checked in on how things were going. We were still enjoying moments of laughter. We were surviving.

This laughter was a surprise to me. How can you laugh or find anything amusing when in pain? They are polar opposites, like sunshine and darkness. Opposites do not occupy the same space, or so I thought.

We went back in to see my doctor a few days after the impromptu surgery to get the pathology report. "Cancer." "It's not that bad." "These are your options." That is all I could hold in my brain at the moment. Thankfully, Delvin had the brain space to keep up with the doctor's words and get us back home. That afternoon was rough as we digested the news.

Amid the fog and fears of the next couple of weeks, laughter again would surface in surprising ways. The neighbor's dogs helped out. Several times a week, one would randomly stick its nose in the air and start howling. It would not be long before the second would join. They were so mournfully off key that it never failed to bring a smile.

While the language barrier at the hospital made things more frightening and frustrating, it did bring laughter as the brave young nurses tried to explain what needed to be done with limited words and at times actions. One of these situations happened when two nurses were trying to tell me I needed to have an enema to prepare me for the hysterectomy. . I was not familiar with the word, so it took some giggles and multiple tries until I understood that I was to have my colon flushed out with water. It was one of those awkward, so-let's-just-all-laugh moments.

Delvin's dry responses to situations around the house helped lighten heavy moments. I don't know how many times tears turned to laughter as he dramatically tackled the kitchen work and cleaning.

Bits of beauty and love brought joy. The flamboyant tree in its full radiant fiery blooms felt like a bouquet from God that lasted for weeks. Nothing cheered me more than to get a message saying, "I'm praying." Nieces and nephews' prayers were extra special. One niece, I guess worried we were missing American cuisine, prayed, "Help them find the food that they are hungry for." Food and flowers dropped off by friends said, "We care" and also broke up the long hours.

There were many days on my journey that laughter didn't bubble from my soul. God was present those days as well and gave the strength needed to hang on until energy and mental space returned enough for small bits of laughter and a smile.

Joy and pain, yes, they can coexist, side-by-side, and what a gift that is.

Conclusion

By Sarah Hilkemann

When my teammate and I lived in a small border town in western Cambodia for twelve months, there were many days when the darkness pressed in heavy.

We struggled with closed ministry doors, oppressive neighbors, and the absence of familiar comforts like running water and air conditioning. I wanted to give up—just about every day—and begged God for release.

On Sunday evenings, we pulled out frozen fruit and local coconut milk to blend refreshing smoothies, then crawled under a mosquito net for movie night. With all the doors shut, we could block out the motorcycles whizzing by and the chaos of the little pop-up restaurant next door. One night, we hit play on a movie called *Moms' Night Out*. The main character and her friends just wanted a peaceful evening together, a break from routine and some uninterrupted conversation. What followed was a hilarious series of mishaps and misunderstandings.

I laughed out loud through the whole movie. Even in the moment, I knew this was a gift. It had been far too long since I had let laughter fill the cracked corners of my heart. Laughter didn't fix that hard season. I didn't suddenly fall in love with small-town border life. It didn't erase the pain of the past, and there were still hard days to come. But that moment of laughter was like kindling, feeding the fire of joy, perseverance, and hope in my soul.

Laughter is more than just a fleeting moment of amusement—it is a gift. It is a thread woven through the fabric of our experiences, a quiet resilience that allows us to keep going when the road is long.

In this book, we've laughed at language blunders, cultural mix-ups, and the unexpected joys of daily life. But perhaps the greatest gift of laughter is how it draws us closer—to the people we serve alongside, to the cultures we learn to love, and to the God who created both humor and joy.

Laughter reminds us to hold things lightly, to embrace the role of learner with humility, and to find delight in the small moments. It helps us endure the difficult seasons and lifts our eyes to the goodness of God, even when things don't go as planned.

There are times when laughter comes easily, spilling over in shared moments of joy. And there are times when it is hard-won, a reminder that we can hold both sorrow and joy in the same hands. The beauty of this journey is that God is present in both—the tears and the laughter, the struggles and the celebrations.

As you close this book, may you carry with you a renewed sense of the joy in your own journey. May you remember to laugh at the unexpected, to delight in the small surprises, and to see humor as a reflection of God's goodness.

And when you find yourself in a moment of awkwardness, misunderstanding, or sheer hilarity, may you pause, take a deep breath, and know that this too is part of the story He is writing.

Meet the Editors

In 2013, **Sarah Hilkemann** left the cornfields of Nebraska for the rice fields of Cambodia, where she made her home in big cities and little villages. In 2018, sensing the Father's push back to the U.S., Sarah transitioned into her role with Velvet Ashes as the Director of Operations. She is grateful to be close to family again while missing her home on the other side of the world.

Laura Bowling spent ten years in cross-cultural ministry, serving in church planting and education in Portugal, South Africa, and Ireland. Between lesson planning and counseling at camp, she made lifelong friendships and explored Europe. She now lives in Southern California with her husband, Chris, and works as managing editor for an international ministry. While she misses the adventure of overseas life, she's thankful that she can continue to use her talents to share the Gospel around the world.

Shaped by her time as a wife, mother, and ministry leader in South Sudan, **Denise Beck** now allows those experiences to guide her in her role as Executive Director of Velvet Ashes. Bringing hope and courage to women as they serve cross-culturally is a role she feels honored to pursue whether through her leadership at Velvet Ashes or alongside her husband as he cares for global workers as the Executive Director of Barnabas International. She and her husband happily serve together from a small village in Southern Wisconsin.

Meet the Authors

Section 1: Laughter Between Worlds

Eva Burkholder was born in Papua New Guinea to missionary parents and later became a global worker herself in Indonesia. Currently she provides member care for Christar. She is the author of *Favored Blessed Pierced: A Fresh Look at Mary of Nazareth*, co-author of *Grit to Stay Grace to Go: Staying Well in Cross-Cultural Ministry*, and blogs regularly at evaburkholder.com. She and her husband live in Texas and enjoy spending time with their family and new granddaughter.

Avery Rose enjoys village life in Central Asia where she works in community health as a speech-language pathologist while continuing to pursue being a lifelong language and culture learner. In her free time you may find her baking bread, crocheting, writing, playing board games, or curled up with an intriguing book. She loves deep conversations, laughing with friends, walking in nature, and contemplative practices.

Together with her husband, **Chris D.** has lived and served in Southeast Asia for over three decades. All three children grew up there, having returned to their passport countries a few years ago but holding fond memories of their growing up years in Southeast Asia. Helping bring the Word to people groups without access in their mother tongue is one of the main burdens on Chris's heart. When time allows, you'll find her with her nose in a book.

Janessa Cypher is a mom of three and serves alongside her husband with Cultivate Discipleship Ministries in Northern Uganda. She has a passion to write of the grace found in waiting seasons and loves to create art whenever she can. However, she is more often found sipping an iced coffee while homeschooling, writing poetry in the margins of motherhood, or nature journaling alongside her children. She enjoys writing for both Velvet Ashes and A Life Overseas. You can find more of her writing at wildernesswriting.blogspot.com or on Instagram @wildernesswriting.

Darlene Grace and her family spent thirteen years serving in Asia. Now serving in the Pacific Islands, Darlene says the two locations are completely opposite in every possible way, but she loves the adventure of serving the Lord with joy, wherever He leads.

Gwen Elm (not her real name) has made South Asia home with her husband and two small children for the last seven years. Gwen works alongside her husband to learn a remote, undocumented language, and they are moving towards literacy development programs for this language group. When not studying and concocting grammatical theories, Gwen can be found sewing, cooking, or trying out something new in their garden.

Caroline Found has been working in North India since 2017 and is still surprised that she is here. After a working life in various spheres, she was 58 when she first went to serve in another nation. Now she helps with English language learning along with support, encouragement, and discipleship to students and faculty alike. She continues to be surprised, delighted, and amazed that she has this privilege.

In 2013, **Sarah Hilkemann** left the cornfields of Nebraska for the rice fields of Cambodia, where she made her home in big cities and little villages. In 2018, sensing the Father's push back to the US, Sarah transitioned into her role with Velvet Ashes as the Director of Operations. She is grateful to be close to family again while missing her home on the other side of the world.

Sylvie Hom lives in the Middle East with her husband and rescue cat. She hopes heaven involves quality boba, getting to wear shorts again, finding out what mortifying language foibles she made on earth without ever realizing, and spending time with as many of her local friends as possible.

Lisa Horn moved to South Africa in 2010, and after two years working in orphan centers, she founded PLAY, Purpose Leadership Adventure for Youth, a ministry that hosts free camps to empower disadvantaged youth to be Christ-centered leaders. When Covid put programs on hold in 2020, she went home to Arizona. Camps resumed in 2023, and she returned to the field but just for a few months each year to host mission teams. They do not take the train.

With a background in social work and twelve years of cross-cultural experience, **Charissa Grace Howes** is passionate about advocating for and journeying with others toward Christ and their Kingdom-calling. Writing, coffee-shop scenes, and lots of grace are what keep her going as she embraces motherhood of two littles and servanthood of the King.

Phyllis Hunsucker has lived in eastern Europe for over half her life now. Ukraine is definitely the home of her heart. She and her family have served in local churches and with orphans. They are now continuing on in the midst of war.

Margaret Kepp served for more than eleven years in India on a church-planting team among high-caste Hindus. Currently in the U.S., she now continues to champion prayer for an unreached people group (UPG) and supports church planters among several UPGs in India.

Gretchen Ketner has spent more than fifteen years living and working in Eastern Europe, first in Ukraine and currently in

Lithuania, where she serves as an English instructor and program director at LCC International University. She is also on staff with The Navigators. She enjoys reading, singing, knitting, playing word games, mentoring young women, hanging out with her black cat, Bennie, and traveling, which still sometimes involves bathroom adventures.

Laurie M. has been serving in the international community since 2004. She has learned five languages to varying degrees of proficiency and lived on three continents—providing many opportunities for cultural faux pas. She and her husband Erik are currently serving with Barnabas International as pastoral care providers for global workers. They have three children who are entering into young adulthood. In her free time, Laurie loves writing, photography, and leaving half-finished projects.

Emmy Lopez lives and works with her husband and two kids in the Arab Gulf. She loves cooking spicy food, bird watching, and early morning runs. She spends part of her day chauffeuring her two children to school but also can be found drinking an alarming amount of tea with Afghan and Pakistani women.

Karis Malone is an Aussie living and serving in Thailand with her Thai family. She married into the culture at 19, started having half-Thai babies at 21, homeschools two of her three children and fosters many more, and after spending more than half of her life in

Thailand, she still experiences cultural mishaps on a regular basis. Karis loves chocolate, music, and writing. She has written a guest blog on A Life Overseas and along with her husband has published a book about his transformation from an Isaan gang leader to a devoted follower of Christ.

MaDonna Maurer lives in Taiwan with her husband, Uwe, a German MK who grew up there. They have three adult TCKs. They co-founded Taiwan Sunshine, a charity that supports and encourages families affected by disability. MaDonna is the CEO of Global Crossroads Consulting, where she helps families transition. She loves to write, drink passion fruit red tea, and listen to the waves crashing. You can find her writing at www.raisingtcks.com.

Rachel Mutesi lives in Far North Queensland, Australia, where she enjoys the tropical climate and drinking in the beauty of God's creation. She has experience serving in Thailand and her home country of Australia and currently works as a school chaplain and at a counseling and member care center for cross-cultural workers. Rachel loves the invitation and hospitality of stories and storytelling and is slowly learning to follow God's lead in her writing journey.

Nathalie grew up in a ministry context in Washington, DC. She used to teach Spanish and Bible in the U.S. Now, she and her husband serve in the Sahel, along with their two children. She enjoys doing arts and crafts with her kids, praising God with keyboard and song, and lately, making homemade pasta. She never could have predicted she would be living in Central Africa, speaking French and learning Arabic but is grateful to God that it feels like home.

Kathleen Pittet lives in Chad with her husband and two daughters. An American by birth, she now feels more at home in France, the country of her husband. She has never lived in one place longer than three years and has spent most of her adult life overseas. She has always loved words and languages and has a degree in linguistics.

Michelle Reyes, PhD, is a professor of cultural engagement at Wheaton College, author of the award-winning book, *Becoming All Things: How Small Changes Lead to Lasting Connections Across Cultures*, and the founder of Success Culture Coaching. She is also a leadership coach at the University of Texas McCombs Business School. Michelle helps leaders in cross-cultural contexts feel aligned, find their rhythm and confidently engage with others. Her work has been featured in *The New York Times*, *The Los Angeles Times*, *USA Today*, *NBC News.com*, and *Good Morning America*. Get a free excerpt of *Becoming All Things* on her website: michelleamireyes.com.

Sarah Marie has been focused on church planting in Central Asia for nine years. She spent her first five years on the field as a single woman until she met her husband a few years ago. They each came from one corner of the world and met in the middle. Now they have a happy little boy and a baby girl. With an emphasis on holistic ministry, focusing on the whole person, body, mind and spirit, they continue to reach unreached people groups and disciple others in order to see the church grow in the most difficult places. Sarah loves to read, especially on rainy days with a cup of coffee, enjoys spending time in nature, and has been writing about one thing or another since she was six years old.

Renee Wassick serves in Northern Ghana and has a heart for relational evangelism, discipleship, and spiritual transformation. She is a mom of two rowdy and creative boys who always make life an adventure. Renee also works alongside vulnerable women and children with a trauma-informed approach to spiritual care. A cup of real coffee or a Coke Zero can bring an instant smile to her face.

Section 2: Joy Comes in the Morning

Alison Bury was born in Tasmania, Australia, and spent her young years dreaming and making up stories of the nations and people that lay beyond the sea. She has sailed to many Pacific Island nations with her work with Mercy Ships, visited Southeast Asia with her work with Reef to Outback, and lived in Papua New Guinea when her husband worked for AusAid. This was all a warmup for the ten years the family spent in Trujillo, Peru, where they planted a little church. They are now nestled back in Canberra, Australia, where Alison works as a counselor, plays with their dog, enjoys a good coffee and writes sleep stories.

Along with her husband and four children, **Lynne Castelijn** has been privileged to watch God do some pretty awesome things among the beautiful Banwaon indigenous people of southern Philippines. An Australian, raised by a South African father and rather proper English mother, she insists she's living proof God has a sense of humor directing her to be a tribal missionary living in an exceptionally remote location for decades. Lynne published her first children's book last year, is working on the next one, and has a memoir almost ready to go.

Linda Crouch and her husband Jim were missionary kids who grew up in Nigeria and later returned to teach in Miango, the same boarding school they attended as children. Their five children were born in Nigeria and schooled there through their high school years. Jim taught sixth grade and Bible for many years and later was the principal. Linda taught music classes and piano lessons. Together they loved developing relationships with staff and families through their forty years of teaching. After Jim passed away in 2008, Linda returned to the school for five more years, helping to develop a community outreach to widows. She's now retired and living near family in Charlotte, NC, where she is thankful for opportunities to help with her former organization.

Nikki Howell has worked in Senegal, West Africa, since 2021 with her husband and three young sons. With a background in speech-language pathology, Nikki is passionate about communication, literacy, and child development, as well as infusing that work with the dignity that can only come from the Gospel. She enjoys both the beaches of Africa and the winter snows of Canada, provided she has a good book or deep conversation.

Natalie Hutchings is a big fan of all things fun and lively. She lives and serves in a remote people group in the Asia-Pacific region. Learning a language and living in a foreign place was never something Natalie imagined doing in her lifetime, but her love for the Lord Jesus compels her, and it turns out she can do it by His enabling. In her downtime you will definitely find Natalie sipping on a cup of tea and enjoying any form of creative arts she can.

Anna Brotherson spent almost a decade living in Bandung, Indonesia, with her husband and three children. They returned to their home country of Australia just before the pandemic struck. Anna now spends her time teaching Biblical Greek at Sydney Missionary and Bible College, writing fiction for children and nonfiction for adults, and soaking up the beauty of Sydney's beaches and forests.

Rachael Kabagabu is a global worker at a boarding school in Kenya. In her free time she enjoys running, drinking matcha and mocha lattes, deep belly laughs with friends, and, on the off chance she can find some snow, skiing.

Kristi A. is an American serving with an anti-trafficking organization in Cambodia, alongside her British church-planting husband. She has been living in Cambodia for seven years and plans to be there as long as the Lord will allow. When not at work or in the community, you can find her reading, sipping tea, crocheting, or having cat naps with her kitty, Gertie.

Lillian Joyce is the author of the blog *Ponderings of a Potted Plant* where she turns everyday experiences into stories. Joyce, born in New York, spent most of her childhood abroad with her family. Following her childhood dream, she worked on the ship *Africa Mercy*, before settling down in West Asia. Using these multicultural experiences, she enjoys writing stories that mix and match different cultural traditions. Aside from writing and exploring, she also enjoys sitting on the couch looking out the window watching the rain drip down the glass while deep in thought. You can visit her on Instagram: lillianjoyce8.

Karen Lubbers-Odel has been living in Uganda full-time since 2011. She is joyfully married to Pastor Moses Odel and involved in church planting, discipleship, training, and equipping church leaders and teachers. Karen originates from southwestern Ontario, Canada, and is grateful for the gift of laughter. Karen loves receiving snail mail, knitting teddy bears, and hosting people for meals.

Rebecca Nolley is a cross-cultural worker, wife, mother of five, teacher of God's Word, and writer. She has lived in Uganda since 2015, where she and her husband, Kent, started Terebinth Ministries. Rebecca is passionate about sharing the love of Jesus and encouraging others to do the same. She has published a women's Bible study called *Shine: Being His Light in Darkness* and continues to write and speak in various formats.

Sara Pascal lives with her husband, Sasha, and their two children, Adela and Miroslav, in the capital of Moldova. They are disciple makers and soccer coaches who want to saturate their community with the good news of the Gospel. They are extremely proud of the response of believers in Moldova to the refugee crisis during the spring of 2022.

Rachel Swan is a wife and mother of three littles who loves inserting random song lyrics into conversations when appropriate, which is often. She has a distinct memory as a six-year-old little girl sitting in a church pew, listening to a cross-cultural worker speak, and fervently praying that God would never make her do that. That little girl would be shocked (and probably a little horrified) at the life she now lives. She first ventured into the world of cross-cultural ministry after college and has lived in four different countries since then. Rachel enjoys spending time in nature with her family, eating good food with friends, and sighing/ cringing/laughing at the antics of her wildly creative children.

Amber Taube enjoys ministry in Southeast Asia with her family of five. They operate a camp and conference center in a rural village, providing local believers with a safe and peaceful environment to worship outside of the city. She is a hesitant homeschool mom getting by on good books, hot beverages, and a whole lot of grace.

Darlene Zimmerman, originally from SC, is settling into her Thai community: attempting to make koy soi, her favorite Thai dish, driving a motor bike, and learning to respond with the proper nod and smile. She and her husband live in Chiang Mai working for Open Hands.

Meet the Artist

Rachel lives in her husband's homeland of coastal Kenya. They met in the U.S., where they became friends, fell in love, and got married very slowly, then had two babies and moved to Kenya very quickly. Rachel will always say yes to coffee dates, nature hikes, art museums, and bookstores. She spends her days homeschooling two teenage boys and would point out that this is not incompatible with the other things she loves to do!

WHEN KIDS GROW UP IN
A HOT CLIMATE

Acknowledgements

This book was a team effort, and we are deeply grateful to each person who generously gave their time, creativity, and expertise along the way.

When this project was just a dream, Rachel, Eva, and Beth came alongside us with their stories and insights—both hilarious and heartfelt. Their ideas and encouragement helped shape the structure of this book from the very beginning.

We are especially thankful to Laura, and to Elizabeth Trotter from Stories Set Free, for their expert editing. Thank you for pouring over each word with care and helping this book communicate clearly and beautifully.

Abby, your artwork captured the very heart of this community. Thank you for designing a cover that we absolutely love!

To Jenny—our go-to person for all things publishing—thank you for sharing your knowledge so freely. Your help with formatting and preparing the final version of this book made it possible to hold this vision in our hands.

We are also grateful to the Velvet Ashes Board of Directors, who ask the hard questions because they care deeply about this community. Kim, Laura, Jenny, Bayta, Carol, Sandi, and D'Arcy, thank you for your support, wisdom, and unwavering cheerleading.

And finally, to the women of the Velvet Ashes community—thank you. Thank you for the stories you've shared on these pages and the lives you share with each other and with us. Your obedience, courage, and joy as you follow Jesus right where you are inspire us daily.

May your joy overflow as you keep on laughing.

Endnotes

1. Miriam Rockness, "Holy Laughter", Reflections on the Art and Writings of Lilias Trotter, June 21, 2020, https://ililiastrotter.wordpress.com/2020/06/21/holy-laughter/

2. Christie Nicholson, "The Humor Gap," Scientific American, October 1, 2012, https://www.scientificamerican.com/article/the-humor-gap-2012-10-23/.

3. B. L. Frederickson, "The role of positive emotions in positive psychology: The broaden-and-build theory of positive emotions," American Psychologist, 2001, https://psycnet.apa.org/record/2001-00465-003?doi=1.

4. "Stress relief from laughter? It's no joke." Mayo Clinic, September 22, 2023, https://www.mayoclinic.org/healthy-lifestyle/stress-management/in-depth/stress-relief/art-20044456.

5. Carpenter, Humphrey (2016). *J.R.R. Tolkien: A Biography*. Harper Collins.

6. Sara Youngblood Gregory, "The Health Benefits of Humor," Mayo Clinic Press, March 28, 2024, https://mcpress.mayoclinic.org/healthy-aging/the-health-benefits-of-humor/.

Velvet Ashes is a community of women serving cross-culturally, doing life together all year round.

There are many ways you can join in!
From in-person retreats retreats to monthly resources and annual online conferences, we work to create space for women serving all over the world to find community, spiritual renewal, and resources for their journey right where they are.

Follow us on Facebook or Instagram or join us in our membership site to be part of this sweet community of women.

Head to velvetashes.com to learn more.

www.ingramcontent.com/pod-product-compliance
Lightning Source LLC
Chambersburg PA
CBHW060128130626
46556CB00006B/2272